# No Fold'em Hold'em

**How to Win with the Little Cards
and Send the Rocks to the Bar**

## D. R. Sherer

No Fold'em Hold'em
(How to Win with the Little Cards
and Send the Rocks to the Bar)
by D. R. Sherer

Library of Congress Catalog Card Number 96-71780
ISBN 1-884466-24-9

Editor and Book Design
Dana Smith

Poker Plus Publications
4535 W. Sahara, #105
Las Vegas, NV 89102

# Table of Contents

# Foreword

## by Bill Akeman, Jr., Publisher
## Gaming Times Magazine

In hometown cardrooms across the nation, on the kitchen tables of America, and in casinos the size of cities, people are playing the fast-paced action game, Texas hold'em. Most of them know that "aces and faces" are big winners. What they don't realize is that you can win big with the little cards — if you know how, when, and where to play them.

That's what Sherer's book is all about: How to win with cards that don't have pictures on them. I like that idea, and it seems to me that nobody else has really paid much attention to it. The "big books" are very precise in delineating strategies for playing a K-Q, but give far less advice on how to play a 6-7. And you know what? I'd rather win with 6-7 than with the big cards!

Why? Because chances are that I'll win bigger pots with those tiny little treasures. Of course, I won't win as many pots as I will when I've got the holy brazils, pocket rockets, or big slick. But then, when I've got high cards in my hand, everybody knows it — and I don't get as much action as I do with my puny threes and fours.

Shearer tells you up front that there's a lot of skill involved in playing little cards to win big pots. Then he digs right in and shows you how to do it. Certainly, not everyone is going to agree with his strategies, but isn't that always the way it is when an author comes out with fresh material? ♣

# Acknowledgments

Linda Johnson, publisher of *Card Player* magazine, gave me encouragement to write this book and recommended my fine editor and publisher, Dana Smith. Thank you.

# Dedication

For *Nelson (Sailor) Allen*

# Introduction

This book is for those of you who have the imagination to do something other than wait for the nuts. (That can drive you nuts, you know.) A whole lot of pious books and prestigious magazine articles have been written advising us to exercise patience and wait for big cards before we enter a pot in Texas hold'em. With so many authors espousing the value of big cards, it's about time that someone speaks on the behalf (and benefits) of playing little cards.

Obviously, this book is not for rocks — unless, of course, they want to learn a new way of looking at their cards. This book is for those of us who intend to win money with the little cards. If the rocks don't like it, they can just go to the bar in a rage.

## Our Motto

There is no such thing as a bad hand.
There are only bad flops.

## Our Other Motto

What the hell — take one off!

This approach is not confined to that ubiquitous brand of poker known as "no fold'em hold'em." It simply means that you can play those little hands for profit, using a specific set of skills which this book will teach you.

Winning with the little cards requires knowing when to *fold'em* as well as when to hold'em. It only *sounds* as though you never fold, because when you win a big pot with little cards, other players tend to make remarks such as, "How could you have called my raise with a hand like that?" Or, "You'll be busted before you know it if you keep playing like that."

You see, the rocks think that you should only win pots with big cards ... but they're *wrong*. You're supposed to win pots with any cards you can. And sometimes — more often than most players might think — it's the little cards that come shining through as big winners.

It takes skill to win with big cards. It takes *even more skill to win with little cards*. That's what this book is all about. ♣

# Chapter 1

# Garbage Players Get Paid Twice

A n average player is no fool. In fact, almost all of the players at a poker table are smart. The rocks have little respect for their fellow players. They seem to believe that anybody who does not play as they do is of lesser intelligence. When a player sits and waits for the nuts, his behavior becomes apparent to the entire table. The ordinary player (and, therefore, the intelligent player) *knows* the rock and does not give him any action.

Many of the ideas in this book are anathema to the rocks and their supporting authors. Their doctrine says that the garbage player throws off more than he receives. Thankfully, their ignorance is our gold mine.

Rocks believe that they have a right to the big cards — after all, they've waited for them and, by God, they're entitled to them! Rocks are due ulcers. The wildest player at the table does not receive *almost* as many big cards as the rock: The wildest player at the table gets *exactly* as many big cards as the rock.

So what? So, the difference is that the wild player gets about two and one-half times as much *payoff* for these good hands. Garbage players rake when their little cards hit ... and they rake when big cards come. The extra chips from the big cards go a long way towards paying for ventures with the little ones. ♣

# Chapter 2

# Garbage Players Win Tournaments

## Or "Please Don't Throw Me in the Briar Patch!"

The defining aspect of a tournament is the presence of short stacks, not the least of which is your own. Tournaments quickly reach a point where players are short-stacked. Even if the structure of the tournament is favorable enough to allow you to start with a reasonable amount of chips, it isn't long before half of the players at each table are under pressure. That pressure is double on the "shorts" because of their lack of chips and the disruption that comes from having suffered a beat or two. You must make decisions during these short-stack times based on premises that are both mathematically and psychologically different from the ones that you make in the ring world. It's a different kettle of fish, a different can of worms.

Rocks play tournaments — and the more the better, I say! They get as far as the fourth or fifth table, curse their luck, tell bad-beat stories, and go home to the bar. Music to my ears!

For laboratory purposes, let's look at a tournament from the eyes of the rock. What's a good little rock to do? He has ground around for a good while, blinding off a lot of chips, perhaps winning a few pots now and then ... but the blinds are up and he's in wonderland. Players make desperate moves on his right and left. No matter how he squeezes his blind cards, they are not what he is "entitled" to see. His chips are short. He has no feel for when his cards are good enough to make a move. He doesn't know which players are likely to defend their big blinds because he isn't in the habit of watching for this. In short, he is out of his element.

Being out of his element, the rock fails to survive to the pay window. Nevertheless, he justifies his day by saying that he went from 20 tables to four, and played five hours before being eliminated. This rationalization brings him back the next day ... without the slightest change in his format. Tournament money comes from the last three seats, not the last three tables. Our rock has no chance of getting to that money.

The attitude of the rock, who insists on playing at a full table, hurts him in tournaments. When his ring game becomes two seats short, he screams. To hear him, you would think that someone had dumped a ton of manure in his front yard. The floorman rushes over to him, thinking that someone has had a heart attack. When the table gets three seats short, the rock refuses to put in his big blind (although, of course, he played yours).

The prize for ninth place in a tournament is one-twentieth the size of the first place bounty. To chop the goods, you want to be in the last three spots. Now I ask you, how in the heck would a rock who has gotten as far as ninth place know how to get to third place? After all, 60-to-90 vital shorthanded decisions are coming up — and he hasn't played a shorthanded game in 20 years!

Tournaments are a matter of imperfect starts. Who is better at this than a garbage player? Read "The Fox and The Farmer," a *Card Player* magazine article by Chuck Thompson that is reprinted in Tom McEvoy's *Tournament Poker* on page 67. Thompson knows what he's talking about. The foxes (the wily players who outwit their opponents at the final table) are the garbage players. The farmers (the victims of those smart foxes) are the rocks. Maybe read it twice; it's that good.

Are garbage players luckier than rocks? Not likely. Are they more intelligent? Maybe, but not so that you could go to the bank on it. The answer is simple: Garbage players win tournaments because they are 10 times — nay, 100 times — more experienced in playing imperfect starts in desperate situations. For example, when is the Q♦ 7♣ worth your entire stack before the flop? I know the answer; the rock does not. In short, the garbage player is in his element in a tournament. He is a fish in water, a fox in the woods, a rabbit in the briar patch. And so he wins.

Who buys in? Tournaments are bought into by 50 percent rocks, 10 percent social players, 10 percent maniacs, and 30 percent garbage players. I include in the rock category those new players who are determined to win by playing better hands, because their actions are almost identical to the rocks. The garbage players are an overlay over those rocks. How nice.

Now, if we can only avoid being tortured by the maniacs! ♣

# Chapter 3

# Failure of the Wave Theory

Prior to the supremacy of the concept of isolation, one of its competitors was what I call "The Wave Theory." In this idea, the action coming around the table was a "wave." You were either in front of the wave or behind it. Obviously, the first person to act was in front of the wave of bettors. The player on the dealer button would be after the wave, even if there was only one player in the pot at that point.

In this plan (no matter what it's called), you should limp in if you are in front of the wave and see the flop as cheaply as possible, because you don't know what the players seated to your left are going to do. If you are seated after the wave (after two or more players have entered the pot), you should be aggressive and raise with most playable hands because of your favorable position. Your raise could even "buy the button," as some authors like to say, because raising might just cause the remaining players, including the dealer, to fold. You try your best to thin the field to your left.

The wave theory has an attractive logic. It allows both the "limp in" and the "aggressive" advocates to be correct. The theory honors the importance of position: You limp out of position, and you raise in position. It provides for deception, since you sometimes just limp-call with fine hands, thus confusing the opposition. All pretty neat, huh?

But it doesn't work. That is, exactly one-half of it works. The after-the-wave play works well. But the first part of the plan — the limping in with good hands early — is a disaster in actual practice.

Suppose you just limp in with this hand from early position:

You usually will see three or four (or more) other players come in, some with a raise, and that will be called twice before it gets back to you. Some players are probably holding "the little cards." The strength of those little cards is less than yours, of course, but not that much less. With enough players in the pot, somebody is going to make something almost every time. If you miss the hand — and you probably will — you will be the one who is chasing. Do you think that the stubborn players sitting behind you will fold their small pairs of tens, or fours, just because you bet out? Don't kid yourself.

That old stuff about betting out *whether or not you hit* is intended for a shorthanded game. If you hit the hand in the typical way, with one ace or one queen (anything better is about 25-to-1), there still will be plenty of players with pairs or draws in the oven, and you will *not* be well aware of it when they hit further. This lack of awareness, except for the flush hit, may cause you to bull the big pair right into a fourth street raise. Superior position will allow the donkeys to kick your rear with two small pair, a double gut draw, a pair with a flush draw, and on and on.

Where did you go wrong? *You let them come in!* When you limp in and even one early player calls, the rest of them come running in like trained pigs. Your positional disadvantage becomes exaggerated with increased competition. Two big cards want the smallest number of opponents. They are injured by multiple players. You needed *isolation.*

Suppose you are playing at a table with 20 other players (yes, it's possible), all of whom call your limp bring-in. On the flop, you make top pair, queens — exactly the fine hand that you were hoping for. You bet out with top pair and top kicker into 20 players. How big are your chances of winning the pot? Tiny!

Suppose you have the same two big cards (and the same hit) in a heads-up game and are the first to act. Again, you want isolation. You want the opposition to pay to chase your better cards ... or else, to let you win *as is.* In the longest and the shortest of games, and in all of those in between, you want isolation.

Limping in early in "the wave" is sufficiently destructive that it does not work in practice. ♣

# Chapter 4

# Isolation Is King

A running theoretical dispute has been going on over the years as to whether a player should bring in his hand for a raise or should just limp in. Authors such as Doyle Brunson have put forth a concept that favors the aggressive bring-in. Mike Caro has proposed the "limp and see the flop cheaply" style of play. (In fairness to him, Caro very carefully listed all the advantages of the aggressive style, and acknowledged that his proposal was tentative.)

In its purest form, isolation means isolating the action to one player — yourself — at which time, the dealer pushes you the pot. As a hand unfolds, getting rid of opponents (making them "pay to play") is of such high value that it overrides all other considerations. Isolation is the dominant strategy in hold'em.

Any time, *any time*, isolation is possible, you should try it. The key word here is *possible*. When it isn't possible, then you need to move on to other strategic alternatives. For example, suppose you are in the little blind holding the A♠ K♦. An early player opens the pot for a raise and four players call. Should you reraise? Do you think that a third small bet will cause any one of them to fold? Probably not, so why try? When isolation is not possible, shift to other tactics, such as limp-and-see. (In the Chapter 10 on no-fold'em games, I discuss other situations in which you may not choose isolation.)

In a usual tight game, you want to play small connectors out of position for reasons such as deception, advertising, shock value, and image. You will not impress the opposition by limping in, so open with a raise. In fact, limping in conveys the message that you have a speculative holding. If you always limp in with speculative hands, you have "educated" your opponents as to your holding and, in the long run, will surely pay for doing so. The price of opening with a raise is small, and the reward is high when you leave them mumbling fifteen bets later.

There are exceptions to the "raise bring in" rule in the no-fold'em games so common at limits up to $6-$12. There, you will be playing pairs that are smaller than jacks, and A-x and K-x suited. Bring in these hands with a call because you want as many players as possible in the pot. Your first level of decision is still *isolation,* but in no-fold'em games, your choice is to *not* try to isolate. Chapter 10, "The No-Fold'em Package," amplifies this concept in depth.

The concept of not giving a free card is an alternative aspect of the isolation principle, a different way of saying the same thing. If there is any chance that a bet will cause an opponent to fold, then you are making a mistake if you don't bet. Isolation also includes check raising on the flop. You check, hoping that someone near the dealer button will bet so that you can raise and put double pressure on the rest of your opponents to fold. The purpose of this device is to eliminate players from the pot, even though you first check.

The isolation bring-in, by definition, also applies to the steal raise. You are hoping to win the blinds without a fight; that is, isolate to zero. In some games, the steal raise will work, and in others, it will not. Use it when you think it will; forget it when you think it won't. This advice may sound simple, but the fact is that many players never try to steal raise, and many others try it all the time ... without considering the mind-set of the big blind. You will be more skillful.

Here is some advice on the steal raise. The big blind is watching players, in turn, as they pass or open. They are entering *his* pot. He views the raise-opener as a farmer would view a thief trying to steal chickens. The big blind is searching for a sign, any sign, that will identify the opener as either a thief or a legitimate bettor. When you are the focus of his attention, *do not look at this big-blind person when you open.*

An unskilled opener will look at his hand *first*. If he finds something good enough to steal with, *then* he will glance at the big blind to see who it is, to see if the big blind is someone that he can steal from. This glance gives the impression that the open is based on *who* is sitting in the blind seat rather than on the value of the hand. That impression is correct, and if the big blind sees it, he will call *because of* that glance! You do not want him to call.

Now, suppose you are the bettor. You want the big blind to make a mistake: You want him to throw away the best hand. You certainly don't want the big blind to make a good judgment call, do you? Looking at him *after* you read your hand gives him a reason to defend. Therefore, it is essential for you to note who is the big blind *before* you look at your cards. Do it every hand.

How about carrying this concept one step further? You look at your cards, find a big pair, and then deliberately look at the big blind for the purpose of implying weakness so as to get his action. Pearls before swine! This is a tough act to pull off, and may well be a step ahead of the competition's level of thinking. Being a level ahead of the competition is just as bad as being a level behind. Furthermore, the extra small bet that you are shooting for is not big enough to warrant the risk of having the enemy play the hand. You still have to win the pot, so forget this play! Note who the big blind is before looking at your cards. Whether you are holding A-A or 2-4 offsuit, put in your raise without any attention to him/her.

Some pots get so crowded that it would be a waste of a bet to try to exclude players. An important poker skill is recognizing the times when isolation is possible and when it is not. No book can teach you this skill. Just be aware that an "isolation decision" will be made every hand that you play for the rest of your life. Be prepared to give it your best shot. If the pot reaches you with five players who have put in two bets apiece, it would take a moron to believe that a one-unit raise will cause anyone to fold. Only A-A or K-K are worth raising with for the sole reason of enlarging the pot, and even that might be a bad choice.

When isolation is not possible, then either call or fold. The importance of isolation creates that situation in which a raise is the correct play ... and a fold is the next-best choice. "Bump it or dump it," as some say. In short, when you enter a pot, your first consideration should be isolation. Only when you do not choose to isolate will you limp. ♣

# Chapter 5

# Pairs Versus Connectors

Every table has players who want to play only cards that are 10 or higher. I call them *soft rocks*. They try to play only the big cards, but have no discretion as to how or when to play them. They simply see two large cards, stick in their bets, and wait for further developments. They usually will call all raises before the flop. Cap it with K-10? No problem! Often, there are about three of these soft rocks at every table. With their presence in the game, it is likely that any flop containing a card higher than a nine will pair somebody. Keep this idea in mind while we compare how you can maneuver various garbage hands against the routine big-card holder.

Two likely holdings for a garbage player are small pairs and small connectors. Let's take a look at each type of hand.

### ♣ The Connectors

You've probably read that the 7♥ 6♥ is a playable hand, and so it is.

Suppose that three players have dumped and the action is up to you. You want to play. Do you bring it in for a raise, or do you just call? You've heard that a "volume" hand should limp in to see the flop cheaply. If you follow that advice, most of your opponents who are holding two large cards (plus some who have only one large card) probably will call you down ... and the blind will be in the pot with a mystery holding.

When the flop comes, it is probable that it will contain a card that is jack-or-higher, and most flops will show two cards that are higher than your 7♥. The most likely way to hit your hand is by making one pair, but you probably have kissed off the possibility of winning with your small pair if you have limped in. The idea that you will win with one small pair is gone: It was gone forever the moment that you came in for a call. To win the hand, you now will need to flop two pair, or a draw for a straight or a flush ... and you will be giving away position and odds to continue.

It is a sin to limp in with small connectors. Limping in says that you are giving up on your chances of winning with the rank of your cards, that you are looking only for the draws. If you are going to play the hand, how can you justify abandoning its most likely improvement?

A while back, a fine author wrote an article for his *Card Player* column saying that no matter what he played, he would rather play it against fewer players because then he would have to beat fewer hands to win the pot. About three months later, this same author wrote an article citing the 7-6 suited as a "volume hand" that "cried out" for multiple players. Well, he had to be wrong in one direction or the other. He was right the first time.

Suppose you were given the following proposition: You play the 7-6 suited. Four players (including you) play each flop. You are guaranteed that with each hand, you will have either a flush draw or an open-end straight draw, *but* you never will be able to win the ranks, the pairs, the trips, and so on. Would you play the proposition? You would always have either eight or nine outs with two possible hits for each one.

The opposition would always have the best possible larger draws, plus some redraws.

The answer is that you should decline the proposition. You will win about 10 percent of the time, less than one-half enough to justify the money that you have in the pot. A player with any pair in the pocket would love to take you on. You probably will not get four-way action for the duration of the hand, and any holding against you will be the favorite. In short, you could not possibly want to play the hand if the draws were all that you could make.

The *only* way that the hand is playable is to have all the added value that is in the ranks: one pair, two pair, an open set. These are the common ways to hit the hand. It follows, then, that if you play it, you *must* protect these rank values. To protect the ranks requires that you open with a raise. So, what has happened to the "volume hand" theory? It never existed! The 7-6 suited is not a volume hand. I'll say it again: The 7-6 suited is *not* a volume hand. You might want to just call with the hand after about four others have already entered the pot, but it is equally valuable to go ahead and raise. Then when you make the flush, the straight, or the bettable pair, it is more likely that you will get the calls that you desire. The flop that you are looking for will not appear to help a "raising" hand; therefore, it is more likely that your opponents will call on the turn and the river.

"Wait!" you cry. "Doyle said that this is his favorite hand and he just calls with it." I say, Doyle was talking about no-limit hold'em. In no-limit, you want to limp in or call a small raise so that you can tap (bet your entire stack) on the flop. He is far more cautious with his advice on limit hold'em. Also, the nature of the limit game has evolved since his fine book (*Super/System*) was written. The larger blinds that are popular today help justify a more aggressive approach.

One point further: Sometimes, when you make the little flush, it can be very painful to find yourself beaten by slightly larger suited cards (say, the 10♥ 2♥) that would have folded if you had opened with a raise. Raise it up!

## ♣ The Little Pairs

Change gears now and look at the small pair, a hand supposedly "related" to the connectors. In reality, they are about as related as King Kong and asparagus. You have:

Three players have folded and it is on you. You have decided to play the hand. You could raise because you have heard that a pair is a slight favorite over A-K and you want to isolate. You could limp-call because you have heard that this is a "volume" hand and you need more chips and players to make it worthwhile.

In no-limit hold'em, you could tap. If anyone called, you might have a fifty-fifty chance to double up. Just because this might be a proper play in no-limit has nothing to do with the correct *limit* play.

Look first at raising with the small pair. You raise and are called by two players, including the big blind. Between them, they rate to have four overcards and, together, they are a favorite to make a pair higher than yours. Their pair will play and will not be bullied out of the pot. You will be able to shoot your way out only if both opponents are on a draw *and* both miss, including the miss of making a pair on the turn and river. If you don't bet, one of them will take a shot and then you cannot call.

You are like the submarine in the WWII movies: Your target is a set. If you hit your target, you win; but if you don't, all you have done is ruffle the water and bring the depth charges on your head. In short, you are exactly where you did not want to be — and you have paid double to do it. You get paid 2-to-1 odds before the flop on a 7-to-1 proposition. Sure, sometimes you will snag the set on the turn or river, and the whole table will buzz and laugh while you rake, but each card is a 22-to-1 shot and you simply are not getting paid for that. The conclusion is that you made a mistake by raising.

What about the limp-call with the small pair? If you call, there likely will be three more players entering the pot, maybe as many as six. You are getting about 3-to-1 odds (and maybe 6-to-1) on your 7-to-1 chance of flopping the set ... not too bad. Maybe your call will go through and maybe there will be a raise. Either way, you are putting in less, on average, to try to make the set. This is your goal — to get more players in for less investment to try to flop the set. If you hit, you can play for the big payoff. If you miss, you might find a way to get value, but you just as easily can fold, knowing that your action has been paid for.

Pairs are nice. They allow you to relax and not be your usual bully. You make the money on the set and you are a spectator when you miss. You can slow down, think cool thoughts, call if you must, and be programmed to dump them if the flop is not what you want. Yes, the small pair *is* a true volume hand. A small pair should be brought in with a limp in order to get more players in the pot — unless you are in a steal position and believe that the big blind is a person who will fold.

That said, there is a time when small pairs should be played the same way as connectors. This occurs when you are in the blind or on the button and several people have entered the pot. Trying to isolate with the connectors would be impossible, and both types of hands make a crying call to see a flop.

Just because the two hands play similarly in this situation does not mean that they have the same goals. The connectors still want isolation, and the pair still wants volume. Do not confuse the similarity of the blind play with the opposite nature of the hands. Even after several people have entered the pot, the connectors can be raised to try to get the blinds out and to set up a credible bluff on the flop. The pair has no business making this raise.

Well, there it is. In limit hold'em, small pairs and small connectors *have nothing to do with each other!* They are at cross purposes. They want different patterns of play. Little pairs are volume hands. Small connectors are *not,* and never have been, volume hands. Your mission is to be as aggressive as your heart will allow with the connectors, and as timid as your brain will allow with pairs. ♣

# Chapter 6

# Two Gaps or One?

Connected starting hands come in four flavorful varieties: no gap (9-8); one gap (9-7); two gaps (9-6); and three gaps (9-5). Since not all gapped connectors are created equal, let's compare them to come to some conclusions.

The traditional suited connectors often are displayed as consecutive cards with no gaps between them, such as J-10 or 7-6. We all know that it is easier to make a straight when the start is no-gap, but what about those starts that are not as perfect, those with one or two or three gaps? Players who are trying to "do it right" have a tendency to play only consecutive no-gap cards, and to completely ignore anything else. This is an error.

I propose that a one-gap hand is as good as, or even better than, a no-gap hand, while the two-gapper is meaningfully worse. Take a look at these two hands:

It is tempting to handicap the above hands, the two-gapper and the one-gapper, as being about equal. The small advantage in the rank of the 8♥ appears to cancel the added straight value of the 7♥ 5♣. This is not so! When a straight draw comes to players who are holding the little cards, they often play them out. After all, the shock value of making the thing is valuable in itself. Rocks to the bar again!

A flop has three cards with which to create the straight draw. We do not want to flop an inside-straight draw that has only four outs; the open-end draw with its eight outs is our goal. To create an open-end draw when you begin with a one-gap start, at least one of the three board cards must fill the single gap, and then one of the remaining flop cards must lodge at either end of the consecutive three cards. If you begin with a two-gap hand, two of the flop cards must fit inside the gap. This is harder to accomplish. You will make 28 percent more straights with a one-gap holding than with a two-gapper. That 28 percent is a difference that is worth considering before you enter a pot.

Obviously, it is even more difficult to make a straight with a three-gap hand, such as 9-5, in which three board cards eventually must exactly fill the three gaps. In one of his books, Bobby Baldwin recommends that you not play a hand that would make both ends of a straight. This advice is the same as saying to not play a three-gap hand. The more gaps, the harder it is to have the nuts. The three-gapper can never be the nuts, with the exception of the A-10, which is played for its rank value; making the straight is an accident.

Out of 1,000 connected starts, you will make a straight by the river approximately as follows:

| | |
|---|---|
| No-Gap | 97/1000 |
| One-Gap | 81/1000 (down 16) |
| Two-Gaps | 63/1000 (down 18) |
| Three-Gaps | 49/1000 (down 14) |

The biggest change in frequency is between the one-gapper and the two-gapper, which gives a more solid reason for playing the one-gap hand and not the two-gap hand. Knowing this information gives me the opportunity to dump some well-known starts, such as 6-9 and 10-7, while occasionally welcoming a few lesser-known items such as 8-6 and 6-4.

A one-gap start has more surprise value than a no-gap start. The enemy can "suspect" a 7-6 much more readily than a 7-5. To my mind, this makes the money potential of the one-gapper *superior* to the no-gapper. On the other hand, the two-gap start has no bigger surprise value than the one-gap start — it merely is a poorer hand. In no-limit hold'em, you might be receptive to the two-gapper because what you are seeking overall is great implied odds; but in limit hold'em, the two-gapper is simply a burden.

Now, let's take it just a bit further. I believe that the majority of hold'em players think that any two cards that are 10 or higher are playable. I see it all the time in the laydowns: K-10 bets it up, K-9 hits the muck. I don't exactly know what it is that makes a 10 playable and a 9 suspect, but by the vote of the populace, this seems to be true.

Let's add this bit of insight to our play of one-gap hands. Assuming that an opponent will play any highcard-10 hand, the smaller of the two likely "enemy" cards is a 10. We never want to match one of the enemy's cards, as this would cripple our hand. Thus, when we play one-gap connectors, we want two cards that are lower than 10. Therefore, the *best* connected hand that we can play — with exactly one gap and without matching the enemy's expected cards — is 9-7.

Ah, there it is! The nuts — The best garbage hand alive! All honor to its name. It is stronger than dirt and almost as good as sex. Sometimes, the 9-7 comes suited ... but when it does, how much of its value is in its suited nature, and how much is in its ranks? Chapter 7 deals with that question.  ♣

# Suited Counts, But Not as Much

Confusion exists in the start value of suited cards. I like my 9-7 to be suited, better suited than not. But how much better? The present poker literature on this "strength" is so splattered that it becomes confusing. As an example, one author discusses the times that you should raise out of position with A-K and A-K suited. The recommendation was to often limp in with A-K offsuit while always raising with the suited combination because it is somehow "stronger" — dead wrong. Another writer's groups reveal a bias in favor of the suited combinations because they are "stronger" starts: No, no, no.

Ace-king is a great hand because of its high card strength, its rank power. A flop with either rank makes top pair and top kicker, and you will do it about one-third of the time. You want all of the lesser cards out of the pot because they may hit in unpredictable ways and thus defeat your fragile — repeat, *fragile* — advantage. You want to isolate, play against as few opponents as possible. Period. Period. Period!

The suited feature of ace-with-suited-card wants many players to build a big pot and possibly get a big payday. It wants to limp in to get as many players as possible in the pot, to get good pot odds. Period!

You cannot do both things correctly at the same time: The betting pattern is different; the goals of the hands are different. Thus, you cannot simply add the suited value to the high-rank value, because to maximize either strength requires an opposite betting pattern. This is also true after the flop. When flush cards come, you usually are on a draw. There are 11 draws for every flush that is complete on the flop. A draw is all that the suited chances realistically can expect as a flop. When the draw comes, the flush nature would like a whole table of checks or single-bet callers so as to pay for the cost of making the draw and to build a big pot when the hit comes. If the turn card is a brick, then the same principles carry over to the river.

Schizophrenia! It's nice to get this hand, but you can't execute both betting patterns because their reasons are at cross purposes. You must consider which purpose is the controlling factor, the rank or the suit. The answer is that the high card feature controls. This is true because the flop helps the rank about one-third of the time, by making top pair. Two or more of your suit will flop only about 10 percent of the time. This 2 1/2-to-1 difference in frequency dictates that we honor the rank feature of A♥ K♥ and harm its suited nature.

Also giving honor to the rank feature is that making an error, failing to isolate it against a hand that can beat the big pair, often leads to a big loss; it costs you the entire pot. The error of raising with A-K suited because of its suited feature is an error of smaller dimension; that is, you may drive out some customers and reduce your win when you hit the hand, but you still win the pot!

Further, a common deceptive play after the flop is to bet or raise with a draw. This deception gets paid by the existence of a larger pot. Therefore, an initial raise with the suited hand is not all bad. An opening raise builds pots. In sum, bet according to the *rank feature* of the hand: raise.

Some authors have said that there is a deceptive value to limping in with a quality hand out-of-position. They will even tell you what percentage of the time to do this. However, the personalities who are sitting at a table are the only variable in how often you should try this type of deception. I say that the advice to *ever* limp in with this hand is dead wrong, but if you have the illogical need to do it, then be sure to raise with the A-K offsuit and do your limp-in with the A-K suited so as to give honor to the multiway pot needs of the suited holding.

The same cross purpose exists in all of the suited starts that we love to play. Say that you start with 7♥ 6♥. Do you want to limp in to see the flop cheaply, or raise to isolate so as to protect the pair if it comes and to give yourself a foundation on which to steal the pot on the flop? The answer (probably raise) lies in position, your opponents, who is in the pot, and so forth. Nevertheless, suited cards want more customers and the ranks want fewer.

Assume that you have 7-6 suited and the flop gives you a pair and a flush draw, certainly one of the flops that you would consider to be successful. You like it. However, the draw wants you to limp in to see the turn cheaply, and at the same time, the rank wants you to bet to protect the pair. Often, there will be no help for either path of action, and the dilemma will carry over to the turn. Your wrist and hand must do something: The bet is on you — you must choose. Bet, to protect the pair.

No-limit is different. There may be opportunities to make a big raise, maybe even an all-in bet, based on the overall strength of the hand — that is, the flush chances added to the rank chances for winning. In no-limit, to describe the suited cards as stronger is correct. The strength of the two features can be added directly in the manner of 2+2. Do not push this no-limit concept onto limit play.

If you have a K-J, you have a K-J. *Play it as such.* Don't play a suited holding into any pots that you would not play unsuited. Raise if that is what you would do with any K-J in your spot. If suit comes into play later in the hand, you are a good enough player to adjust to it.

This concept is true in the middle positions, and late, too. If you think that you can steal the blind with a 2-3, go ahead and try it. If your cards are suited, fine; but you still are playing a 2-3! The reason that you attempt the steal is that your evaluation of your chances for pulling it off dictate that you should try it. Period. If you believe that you cannot buy the blind, for whatever the reason, then being suited is never enough to change your decision. Do you think that a bad move with a deuce-trey offsuit is somehow converted into a good move because your cards are suited? No way. In limit hold'em, being suited counts, but not nearly as much as some would lead you to believe.

Chapter 24 on minimum starting hand requirements (appropriately placed at the end of the book) does *not* have a separate chart for suited hands. This is why: There is no time in limit hold'em when being suited adds enough value to a high-card open to make an action correct that otherwise would be wrong.

Note that there is a time when you *want* to play some hands because of their suited potential. I am speaking of the A-x suited and the K-x suited, hands with which you can limp in a no-fold'em game (see Chapter 10). In this case, you are playing the hand primarily for its big-pot flush chances, with the ranks as a bonus. This specialized play does not alter the proposition that being suited does not change any decision that starts with the rank of the cards. ♣

# Chapter 8

# The 2-3-4-5

Not all garbage is created equal. Recall for a moment those *Star Trek* episodes when our heroes entered a parallel universe in which there was an evil Kirk and Spock. Or take an imaginary trip through the looking glass. The concept of an "evil twin universe" is alive and well in hold'em.

The ace, king, queen, and jack (some players also include the 10) are thought to be "good" cards: In pairs, they are a premium start; they can give you an overcard-out; and they are viable kickers. Their high-card nature also provides protection against counterfeiting as a hand develops ... and on and on.

Are there parallel holdings at the bottom of the ranks, whose presence can kill the value of a hand? Yes. The deuce, trey, four, five and sometimes the six, carry this quality. It is the bottom four as opposed to the top four. Their pairs are counterfeited too often. Their kicker power is reduced to zero with the deuce. As the curve of highness bends upward to infinity with the ace, so does it bend downward to infinity with the deuce. The three cards attached to the ace and the three cards attached to the deuce are on a sharp slope of this curve.

We don't want to gamble with the worst of it — we simply want to know the percentages so that we can fire a torpedo into the rocks now and then. It is a question of percentages, position, and psychology. The advice to the garbage player is to be aware that the nine, eight, seven, and six are superior to the two, three, four, and five. This may sound simple, but it is easy to ignore in the heat of battle. Rocks, of course, could care less.

I do not say that you cannot play the smaller garbage cards, just that you should play them less often and with great selection. When you open your hand and see one of those four babies, or their pair, have a good reason before you enter the pot. (You can see the bias against these four smallest cards in the minimum starts listed in Chapter 24.)

Playing small cards is in fashion these days. You may be surprised at how often the eight, seven, or six will out-kick, or out-pair, smaller cards at the showdown. Many chips move one way or the other on these cards. Second-best is expensive. Try to be on the better end of it. Compare these two hands:

A careful reading of *Super/System* brings a gem: Brunson would rather play his suited ace with a wheel card because of its additional straight power, the chance of making a wheel. I accept his advice for no-limit hold'em. A flush draw with an overcard gives 12 outs. The wheel draw brings it to 15 outs. The three-out difference may justify a tap on the flop. Fifteen outs *twice* is nothing to sneeze at. Just ask any no-limit player about fifteen-outs-twice and see him sputter to describe the deadly battle in the offing.

However ... however ... *however:* In the limit game, the A-7 is miles ahead of the A-2. In limit poker, we cannot get properly paid for our straight chances. We *can* get paid for the power that lives in the seven.

The following pairs of hands are an illustration. The cards in the left column are *much* more playable than those in the right column. Many times, both columns are garbage, and are folded without a thought. Many times, they play. One ace or one king is sometimes enough, especially during desperate times in tournaments. In the stealing circumstances, the catch-a-stealer times, the raise-to-isolate instances, the blind situations — you need a good grip on the large differences between the "good" left column and its poor mate.

| Column One | Column Two |
|:---:|:---:|
| A♥ 7♥ | A♥ 2♥ |
| K♠ 8♦ | K♠ 5♦ |
| Q♥ 7♣ | Q♥ 4♥ |
| J♣ 8♥ | J♣ 5♣ |

Oh, the eight plays? Push the sherbet to Herbert! ♣

# Chapter 9

# The Baby Paints: Take Care!

The best swordsman in the land need have no fear of the second-best swordsman. He should fear the dolt who, never having held a blade before, picks it up with two hands and swings it like an ax. In the poker world, the biggest loser is the second-best hand. Some cards are a setup to be second best. Let's try to not be.

High card standards are predicated on the likelihood that you will make top pair on the flop. This spot is somewhere mid-queen; that is, the median flop will show a queen as the high card. Most poker authorities propose raising with a pocket pair of jacks because they are close enough to 50 percent to stand up as an overpair, or maybe top set, on the flop. Likewise, the A-J is the minimum approved high hand to play out of position because the total package is favored, on average, to create top pair: the ace for certain, possibly the jack, and either with an appropriate kicker.

As currently dispensed, the above advice leaves some players with the impression that all four top cards — the ace, king, queen, and jack — are "high" cards with strength enough to be played. They err.

The difference between the playability of the high-card hands is the "less helpful kicker" factor. In the A-J example, the ace kicker helps you when you make a pair of jacks. The jack helps you when you make a pair of aces because of the tendency of many players to play almost any hand with an ace in it, thus making your jack a favorite to be the best kicker.

The three hands without an ace — K-Q, K-J, Q-J — are not as blessed. Players who enter pots with a king or a queen often set higher standards for kickers, making the median kicker for these hands far higher. The jack is not as much help for the king as it is for the ace. The king is not as much help for the jack as is the ace. Trouble really starts for queen and jack hands. Note that Chapter 24 on minimum starting hands lists only unpaired-*ace* hands starting in the first three positions down to A-J. King-queen just doesn't cut it.

Now, if the median high card on the flop is the queen, then to have an advantage, one needs better-than-average cards to get the goods. Better than average means an ace or king. By way of parallel thought, a pair of aces or a pair of kings is enough to tap (go all-in) in no-limit action. Why not queens? Because a pair of queens must survive two overcards, whereas the kings need fear only one overcard, a 100 percent difference in rank vulnerability. A 100 percent difference is a monster figure in a world in which major decisions are tied to small margins.

The same principle is true for one queen: It need fear twice as many overcards as its higher mate. The point is that aces and kings are the only big cards — no others are. Hands with a queen or jack in them can be sirens luring you into murky waters for some second-best action. The call may sound the loudest when you are in the blind, where the appearance of a face card may cause an illogical temptation to make your blind good. But remember: The second-best swordsman went to the cemetery. Any time you are playing a queen or a jack or a 10 without an ace, you are in a dangerous situation ... maybe too dangerous to be a money winner.

The garbage cards, nines and below, are somewhat protected by the smallness of their ranks. The ace and the king are somewhat protected by their bigness. This line of reasoning leaves the queen and the jack (and maybe the 10) as *pseudo big cards*.

The king and the queen sort of "feel" as though they have a lot in common: They are connectors, they are together as paints. But maybe it's time to imagine a big line — a big gap — between them.

A♠K♣ —————————— Q♥J♦10♠ —————————— 9♦

My tentative proposition is this: The baby paints — the queen, jack, and 10 — *without an ace* — are money losers when they are played for top pair. They constitute a trap by giving you the *illusion of bigness,* just enough to get you involved, before the pot is snatched away from you.

What about all of those draw possibilities with queen, jack, and 10? A *big* flush is one headed by an ace or a king. These three impostors are just big enough to cost an extra bet or two in a *losing* pot. The straight draw is clean; however, it is hard to make and sometimes gets beaten by a flush.

Long-term results are difficult to see when you are involved in a pot. Give these three traitors a careful eye when you invest. Put the same money into something prudent, something proven, something solid — such as a bring-in raise next to the dealer after pretending to look at your cards. ♣

# Chapter 10

# The No-Fold'em Package

No fold'em hold'em games are everywhere: You can't avoid them even if you try. Pots are played by five, six, seven, and eight players. There probably is a dealer or two playing in the game (the only thing sweeter is having a floorman in it). Raises mean next to nothing. You have no idea which cards your opponents are holding and the flop is immaterial to their actions. The idea of manipulating the enemy is a fool's errand. Isolation does not exist — No-fold'em hold'em at its best!

Games also often have a business person who just came from work still wearing a white shirt. Such corporate people don't have enough energy left to play good poker. (Dealers just off duty are in the same pitiful situation.) Not only are many of them inexperienced players to start with, but they are tired and often play softly against each other. This phenomenon is the basis of:

## "Sheriff's Law"
$$P = W(2)$$
"Profitability is equivalent to the number of white shirts squared."

The no-fold'em table is different, and we need different tools to beat it. As my old friend Sailor Allen used to say, in poker, one adapts to the conditions that prevail. The first order of business in no-fold'em is to think *big pots*. We want hands that beat other *good* hands. This means having a big flush, or a set/full house. To get to the set/full house goal, we will play all pairs. To get to the big flush, we will play A-x and K-x suited. With these holdings, we limp into the pot.

Poker is a zero sum game. "Zero sum" means that when one side is helped, the opposite side is hurt. In poker, if one holding goes up in value, then another one necessarily decreases in value. If the holdings discussed above are helped in no fold'em games, then which ones are harmed? Let's take a look at four types of holdings.

## ♣ Two Big Cards

Two big cards are the big victims. Their former plan was to make top pair with top kicker, and perhaps intimidate some poor soul if they didn't hit. No chance for that now. Intimidation is a joke and top pair is exactly what one of the enemy wants you to have. Unfortunately, two big cards is what we have been taught to play. This isn't to say that you can never play them: Just proceed cautiously.

In a no fold'em game, somebody almost always holds whatever is on the board. For this reason, the concept of making second or third pair, then betting to isolate, will not work. Second pair, no matter how large, should be routinely checked and folded.

## ♣ Big Pairs

Big pairs (aces and kings) are injured. If they do not make a set, they are in danger, just as is the A-K with one hit. Further, if one of your opponents is holding a pocket pair, the flop gives him three chances to help instead of two. Straight and flush players are a good deal more dangerous. Recall that a big pair wants you to raise on every occasion before the flop to eliminate players, and thus to lessen the chances of the open set, the small two-pairs, the draws, and all of those things that kill a big pair. You still want to raise, but your chips simply are not as well spent. In the no-fold'em setting, the big pair's through-ticket quality does not exist; its ability to win on its own is about one-third of what it is in a tight game. Big pairs are damaged.

## ♣ Drawing Hands

Straight draws may appear to be helped in no fold'em games because they get a bigger pot for the investment. On the other hand, it is not good to put in two, three, and four bets when the rank of your cards is of little help. Further, the multiplicity of players makes flushes more common, which is bad news for straight draws. Second-best is a bad loss. Call it even for the straight draws.

Flush draws are helped in no-fold'em games, with the warning that two, and sometimes three, people make the same flush. Thus, *big* flush draws are helped; small ones are hindered.

A king is sufficiently ahead of the average opposition that a king-high flush is, overall, a big winner. Sure, there are times when your king flush has gotten kicked in the fanny by a slow-played ace, or a fourth flush card on the river. But when you add up all the wins and subtract all the losses, the king-high flush is still a big winner.

## ♣ Little Pairs

Ah ... here are the clear gainers. Small pairs now get the necessary 6-to-1 odds in the pre-flop action alone. From there on, all is pure gravy. If you don't make a set, it is no big loss; the hand has been paid for. When the set comes, it wins giant pots from the big cards. It wins giant pots from the flushes and straights when there is an innocent-looking pair on board. (Strangely, in no-fold'em, the presence of a pair on board is but a small deterrent to the flush players. They bet out just to see if they will get raised, and then call when they do.) The slight danger to pairs comes from a higher pair. Of course, set over set is a known item. The point is that little pairs are big,

*big* gainers in the no-fold'em arena. They can be played in almost any situation for any number of bets.

## ♣ The No-Fold'em Package

From the preceding discussion, we can develop a "package" to insert into no-fold'em games. This package consists of all the small pairs, and the A-x and K-x suited. The following three hands, the deuces representing "any small pair," are the No-Fold'em Package:

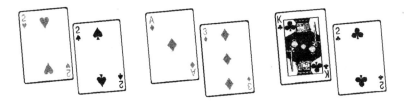

These are true volume hands. We want as many players as possible in the pot; therefore, these hands are played limply. Enter for a call. Call a bet. See the flop as cheaply as the opposition allows.

When you hold one of the top four pairs, you still need to try to eliminate players with a raise. Although raising is not as successful as it is in other games, you still may eliminate one or two players who might just hold that lonesome king that will kill your pair. You will limp out of position with nine ranks of pairs, the 10s through the deuces. As you approach the dealer button, the smaller pairs and the single high card would generally qualify for a raise, but in no-fold'em, you don't get the chance.

You are dealt a pair once in seventeen hands. You will limp in with the smaller pairs one out of every 29 deals. This frequency is similar to the frequency with which you will receive the A-x and K-x suited. Putting them together, the en-

have no idea about what you are holding when you limp in. If you only limp in with small pairs, they would easily pick up on that. The limp with two big suited hands (the K-x and A-x) is not only desirable, it is an essential mask to the play of the nine small pairs. The necessity of providing cover for the small pairs outweighs any imaginary fear of playing a "small" king. Do not cower!

Some "play-like-a-rock" authors have given bad press to the A-x suited; perhaps they refuse to admit that no-fold'em hold'em exists. I go in the other direction: Always play K-x suited, regardless of position, in a no-fold'em arena. You will be surprised how infrequently you lose to the ace-high, and how often you make a fine hand by accident with the king-high holding. Note also those times when the ace of your suit flops. Most no-fold'em players will play any ace. This gives the king holding exactly what it wants ... lots of customers. Do not fear the king. It is part of the game plan.

The second half of the no-fold'em formula is to dump all but the very best unpaired and unsuited hands out-of-position (Recall that these hands are injured in the no fold'em arena.) Thus, when you are out of position, dump K-Q, K-J, K-10, Q-J, Q-10, J-10, and anything worse.

Great patience is required in no-fold'em games ... the patience to discard all of the non-pair big cards out-of-position. Note: This is very hard to do when it's the middle of the night, you're in a "good" game, and you're stuck. In Chapter 22, "The Maniac and the Little Cards," I explain "good" games further. Just believe that for garbage players, "good" games are tough to play and "bad" games can be very profitable.

## ♣ When to Use the No Fold'em Package

When is a game ripe to insert the no-fold'em package? Good question. Several writers have created "counts" or formulas by which to grade a game ... sort of a cookbook approach. I find these formulas unworkable, since mortal players are concentrating on other things. You will *know* when the game is no-fold'em: Your instincts are good enough.

What about those games that approach no-fold'em status, but are not quite there? In games that are on the borderline of being no-fold'em, loosen up on your play of pairs and clamp down on unsuited cards out-of-position.

There is an old story about obscenity. One justice said that he knew it when he saw it, but he didn't know how to define it. The same applies to a game that is loose enough to insert the no-fold'em package. If you think that it's time to start putting in four bets with deuces from first position, do it. A set is a set, and it knocks the you-know-what out of aces-up. Patience, knowledge, and the no fold'em package will overcome these games. ♣

# Chapter 11

# To Defend Or Not To Defend

Decisions that happen often are important. Whether to defend in the blinds is one of them. Twice each round of the table, you play the blinds. Garbage players tend to defend. Therefore, this defense becomes a big, *big* bankroll item that deserves special attention and care.

According to the statistics put forth by Mason Malmuth (*Poker Theory and Other Topics*), a winning player can play for a year and still be in the hole. I believe him. Likewise, a losing player can play for a year and show a profit. The margins are that thin. Keeping these figures in mind, it would be impossible to get a good feel for whether you are playing the blinds correctly based on how you did this hour, day, week, or month. There is nothing in the results that you get from defending/not defending that will tell you whether you are doing it right.

Nevertheless, garbage players tend to defend with seemingly insane holdings because "the price is right." And we love to swim upstream. One half of a small bet in the little blind or one small bet in the big blind appears to be a small price to pay. Say that we get three-and-one-half odds — who could pass that up? If we miss, we are going to check and fold. If we hit, we're going to bet out and terrorize the table. Right? Wrong!

I know a player who has supported himself at hold'em for 20 years. He almost never completes his little blind, and puts in the big blind call only about one-sixth of the time. He simply doesn't want to enter an arena where he must make plays with imperfect cards. It isn't his style. Nevertheless, he is eating. Blind defense is a luxury. It is something that we should do for image, shock value, or recreation — but *not* for profit.

In his farewell address to the Corps of Cadets at West Point, General MacArthur said that when death approached, his final thoughts would be "... on the Corps, on the Corps, on the Corps." If a garbage player is using good timing, using good psychology, and still cannot win, then the first three places where he/she should look for the leak is the blinds, and the blinds, and the blinds.

Some theorists have stated that the position deficit in the blinds is partially made up for by their lower price. This poor advice becomes a trap for little-card players because we use it to justify playing almost anything in the blind. The sad truth is that starting a hand in the blind is a mistake that worsens in geometrical proportion as the play develops. It is not just a little bit more — It is the entire betting pattern that will follow. You are not putting in chips just to lose them, you want to play out the hand. *The "bargain" offered by the blinds is not nearly enough to make up for the losses that probably will occur on later rounds.*

When you are in the blinds, you want the pot to be raised when it gets to you; in fact, you *need* the pot to be raised. The reason for this is the information that comes with the bets, and the smaller number of players that you have to deal with. A raised pot is just what you want, as you will read later in more detail.

## ♣ The Small Blind

The small blind is a pretty dull item: It is nowhere, trash adrift in a smelly river. Here's the problem: The bet comes to you either raised or not raised. If the pot is raised, then the discount that is given by the small blind is not enough to sway your decision. If you call, you are just putting in a big bet out of position. If you have a hand of very high quality, you play it ... but who didn't know that? If the pot is not raised, you have a bargain, one-half of a little bet to see a flop.

However, this "bargain" is no bargain! You are out of position with poor cards; you know absolutely nothing about what the opposition is holding; and worst of all, there are too many of them to use isolation as a weapon. To add insult to injury, the big blind could do something stupid like raise the pot. You have no tool to work with! Paradoxical as it may seem, to play the little blind in an unraised pot, you need some sort of quality cards. Cure that knee jerk (or is it a wrist jerk?) reaction to toss in one more chip.

Just during the little blind, pretend that you are a rock. Ugly! Throw away a lot of hands in the small blind — it will do your soul good. There is a technique to doing this: Think about discarding *before* you read your hand. This mental advance will help to cancel the automatic temptation to play. (In *Tournament Poker,* Tom McEvoy writes about the deleterious effects of "reflexive actions" in tournaments. Don't make automatically calling from the little blind one of yours.)

The only sunshine in the little blind is that the limp play required is consistent with how to play a draw hand for its *draw value only.* Perhaps a case could be made for calling in the small blind only with suited cards. (Think about it ...)

### ♣ The Big Blind

The big blind is where the action is. It has been said (and correctly so) that if nobody raises the blind, then somebody has made a mistake. The big blind gets a free flop — thank you very much! When this happens, the opposition has sort of given you an entire free round. Nonetheless, this bargain comes with defects ... three of them, in fact. There are too many opponents; you are out of position; and you have no intelligence

48

information. These are *not* small matters. Together, they are one *big* matter.

If you are in the big blind and nobody raises, do the following: (a) Pinch your nose at their gutless play; (b) Read your cards with a paranoid eyeball; and (c) Proceed in slow motion.

You need a better hand to join the betting after a free flop than you do when the pot has been raised. For free, you want the nuts. You probably will not get that perfect flop or anything close to it. So, be mentally ready to realistically read that flop, and then save your best tools for another hand.

They raised your blind? Well now, this is more like it. The battle is on! Get me in the castle and I'll think of something. Who raised it? Who called? Who didn't reraise? How many of the enemy are there? Who glanced at the big blind? Who glanced to his left? Who acted weak while jumping the fence? Yum. Yum. Yum.

With all of this information, it is almost impossible to be holding two cards that are not worth one small bet. Your call gives away no information whatsoever as to your holding. If only one or two enemies are in the pot, you will later isolate and win with the smallest of help. If there are three or four of them, the increased number of chips in the pot makes your information that much more of a bargain. I have gone for hours without missing a one-bet call on the big blind. It's almost like a required ante.

One caution: Do not reraise in the big blind position unless you are holding A-A or K-K or, maybe, connectors to disguise the big pair. Why? Because isolation is not possible at that moment, and the table is already sure that you have nothing. They know that you defend your blind with "nothing." You are in a great spot to do some real slow-play damage if you flop a set of queens, for example, or top pair with top kicker. Why give them any free information — make them pay later. ♣

# Chapter 12

# An Out-of-Position Play

O K, there you are, a graduate garbage player. You're
in a game with several players in the pot. You have
just called a raise to defend your big blind with:

The flop comes 10-6-5. You have flopped a pair of fives! Not
too bad; after all, it *is* what you came to the party for.

You bet out. You *have* to bet out. If you don't bet, you
will let all those players, each one probably holding one of the
four big cards, in for the turn. And you know that it probably
will hit them. Further, if you don't lead out, you can bet your
last chip that they will bet, and then you almost cannot call.
You bet out.

A couple of players muck their hands. Close to or on the
button, a certified died-in-the-wool rock raises. Another player
dumps, and then it is back to you. What to do? What to do?
There is an *exactly* correct answer — or more precisely, a pair
of exactly correct answers.

For starters, we can estimate what the rock is holding. He
doesn't have two pair, because he never would have played
two of *those* cards to begin with. He could have a set. He

could have an overpair. He might have an ace with the 10. No other combination really belongs. But wait a minute: *Wait a minute!*

He could have a suited ace. You know that he has read some flummery that raising with this holding will "buy" him a "free card" on the turn (almost nonsense), and he believes it. Lucky for you, the chance that he holds the suit is just about as big as all of those other holdings combined! You are alive ... *alive.*

So, what you do is this: Look to see if the flop contains exactly two cards of a suit. If the flop *does* contain exactly two of a suit, you:

(a) Call the bet;

(b) Be prepared to bet out on the turn if neither the ace nor another suited card appears;

(c) Be prepared to check and call (his hapless bluff) on the river if the ace or the suit does not appear.

If the flop *does not* contain *exactly* two of a suit, you:

(a) Announce loudly that you have misread your hand *again*!

(b) Pick up your garbage so that the players at your end of the table can see your cards — see that you defend with garbage, and see that you will bet with it, too.

(c) Toss it in the muck. ♣

# Chapter 13

# Lead With Your Hits

S uppose you play, and perhaps even raise before the flop, the most excellent hand of:

You have taken the shot. The flop comes and you take off one of your cards, say it is the seven. A one-pair hit is the most likely way that you will hit the hand. It's what you wanted. It's what you played for. What do you do next? Just as in the play described in Chapter 12, you bet.

If you are the first to act, bet it out on the flop. If someone bets in front of you, raise. The price of the raise is one small bet, peanuts in comparison to what has gone on before, and what may come later.

If the opposition has nothing — and most of the time, they will have nothing — you might win the pot right there. If they have something, they will let you know. On the turn, you might get lucky and hit your kicker, or even make a set. What you came for is a large pot, so the extra bet serves this purpose, too.

On the other hand, if you do *not* bet, then all sorts of bad things happen. First, someone may take a shot at *you*, especially if there is a scary looking overcard, such as a queen, on the flop, in which case you may have to fold the best hand.

Second, if the opposition has a couple of big cards, the turn may hit one of them. Since three or more opponents probably have paid to see the flop, they must have some kind of a hand, probably an assortment of cards 10-and-up. In fact, this is exactly what you should expect them to be holding. Just about any card higher than your seven, except for a nine, is a spear in your heart. You simply must try to make those single big cards hit the dirt on the flop.

Third, your bet is defensive insurance in case the board shows two of a suit other than yours. If a third suited card comes on the turn, you can check and still be credible enough that you will not get bet into on the river.

Note that we are talking about betting a small pair, one that is below a jack in rank, regardless of whether it is top pair on the flop. In Chapter 18, "Deception on the Flop," I discuss several psychological factors that may influence your betting decisions, factors that may or may not cause you to bet out on the flop when you make top pair. Lead with your hits. ♣

# Chapter 14

# Drive at Suited Flops

It would be nice if all your opponents played like rocks. They don't. The first thing that maniacs and other aggressive types do is barge into pots where they don't belong. The second thing they do is to get really aggressive with their flush draws, which is the focus of this chapter.

Although some players become aggressive with a straight draw, it is more common to see a swarm of kamikaze bets come in when the flop shows a couple of small diamonds. In my experience, players use unwarranted aggression with flush draws about six times more often than straight draws. This is justification enough to treat the flush aggression phenomenon in its own category.

**Flush Draw Betting Pattern.** The betting pattern of players on a flush draw is distinctive. They raise on the flop, put in a reraise when possible, and perhaps even cap the betting. On the turn, they bet if they hit, or check if they miss. On the river, they quietly fade away. The enemy's thinking is to give as much shock value to the flop as possible, and then to get value on the turn or a "free" card on both the turn and the river.

**Straight Draw Betting Pattern.** There is a different pattern to the aggressive betting of a straight draw. The straight-draw player often checks on the flop, or if he bets it, he continues to bet on the turn and the river, in the manner of continuing a bluff. Your ability to detect clues from his body language is your protection against the straight draw. If you believe that it's a gambit, call him down. Be sure to tell the table about your defense afterward. When you are defeated, show your medium pair, saying "Well, it worked the last two times."

The player on a flush draw bets big on the flop. He hopes to keep right on betting when the hit comes. He wants a big pot to guarantee action when that hit comes. The player on a straight draw doesn't need a big pot because his hit is not as visible. He can check on the flop, make a cheap hit, and then bet out with hopes of getting some play from his opponents. The flush hit is transparent, and the table is stilled by the presence of three suited cards on board. The big flush push on the flop is an expected play. We must adapt to this play ... and use it to our advantage.

**Playing Garbage Cards.** When playing garbage cards, we want immediate help, *flop* help. Without it, the game is over and we wait for another hand. Skill comes into play when we hit a good hand, sometimes something nice: a little set, an open set, two pair. We know that if we make a small pair, we will bet out, but there are all of those other and bigger hands — we, too, make a set now and then!

Suppose you flop a set or two pair and it is your turn to bet. On what do you base your decision? I recommend that the controlling factor be the nature, the suit texture, of the board. If the board shows exactly two of a suit, it is (by my definition) "suited." If the board is indeed suited, do not slow play and do not check raise. Bet out! All of those dolts with flush draws will jack it up *for* you. Two little bets are as good as one big one.

Further, your bet is standard in that you want to make them pay to see the next card. Even the rock, praying for a free card, is frustrated when you lead out. For example, consider the open set, a hand that garbage players see a lot of on lucky days.

You started with 8♠ 6♠ and the flop comes:

Many players have a tendency to slow play this holding, hoping to set up a check raise on the turn. Such a play may raise returns, but it also maximizes danger. A slow play with an open set is a close call, anyway. The presence of the diamonds is too much for the slow play to bear. When you see a suited flop, bet out; the returns are sure to come. Just pray that a suited card also hits your kicker. Your bet-out will be read first as a bluff; second as a king; and only third as a set. You will find the correct path to make the flush draw pay you.

There is a second and equally important reason for leading at a suited board. When the third suited card hits, it doesn't always make a flush for someone. If you previously bet at the board when it showed two of the suit on the flop, you can check on the third flush card and still maintain your credibility. From the enemy's eyes, you could be holding as big a hand as top set and still correctly check to the three-flush. However, if you check on the flop, and then check again when the suit hits, the enemy will be very certain to bluff at you since you apparently didn't have enough to bet with before the third suited card hit the board. You never want the enemy to bluff you, so prevent it by always betting at a suited board.

If there are two of a suit on board, you simply cannot hold a hand that is big enough to slow play. All slow plays, the check raise, the smooth call, are to be done *only* if the board is not suited. ♣

# Chapter 15

# Uniform Flops:
# The Kiss of Death

D oyle warned us about uniform flops. They are dangerous environments for our small cards to venture into. If it is true that only isolation will protect the small cards, then we want to be playing in pots that opponents can be driven out of. One of our worst nightmares is a flop such as:

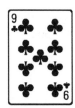

A maximum number of players will have reason to stay in the pot against this type of flop. Some of them will race to see who can cap it just to disguise their draws. We might be playing that very fine garbage hand:

In an insane flash, we begin to think that we can win with second pair and the bottom end of an open-ended straight draw. Forget it! We probably are dead already, and on the slim chance that we are still alive, we have only three outs, any one of which could wind up in a split pot. The enemy has no end of redraws. Isolation is impossible. There is no way out except the muck pile!

Incidentally, standard advice says that a pair with a straight draw is a weaker hand than it seems to be. This is a problem that does *not* go away with the smaller cards. There are enough garbage players that if you make your second-pair, it too often also will make the opponent's straight. The result is that if you hit your kicker, you may create an expensive loss to a straight. The power in the ranks is essential to a winning position, and you simply cannot afford to have no kicker. Heed the advice: Uniform flops are the kiss of death.

The rock who is in the above pot may still have a chance. He may be playing:

With this holding, the rock has the top gutshot straight draw, two overcards, and the queen of trump. He may be chasing on the flop, but he does have outs. Recognize that we do not have outs, and release the hand.

Obviously, this flop example is the worst-case scenario, but the principle remains the same. A uniform flop hurts the garbage cards — and it hurts them *more* than it hurts the big cards. Unless the flop is perfectly tailored to your holding, a uniform flop is the signal to waste no chip. ♣

# Chapter 16

# Board Pairs: A Stab in the Heart

Cousin to the uniform flop is the board pair. Mike Caro is on the mark in advising that when the board pairs, it is bad news for you unless it helps your hand exclusively. This is even *more* true as it applies to the play of small cards.

Obviously, the pair hurts your ability to run down a larger pocket pair; but it hurts you in other situations, too. To see the validity of this concept, compare what happens to these two hands that are being played in the same pot:

Sitting next to the dealer, you brought it in with a raise. The little blind reraised; you just called. Eight small bets are in the pot. The flop comes:

Both you and the A♣ J♣ have a pair with a live kicker. You have a gutshot draw at the straight, giving you a total of nine outs. On the turn, the board pairs with the 10♣.

You have just lost your kicker! Now you're looking at six outs instead of nine. This three-out loss means major damage to your position. You knew that you had the worst of it, but that was "normal" for you. You needed your kicker to be ripped off like you needed a hole in the head. The big blind still has a live kicker. The board pair has damaged you exclusively.

What's worse is that you now must fear the possibility that the enemy has a pocket pair or a 10. His reraise before the flop tends to say "No 10," but you can't be certain since you know that some dolts will always raise with A-10 or J-10 suited. Your ability to isolate has suffered a terminal hit.

If the enemy has the J-10 or the A-10, you are almost certainly dead. Psychologically, the board pair has damaged you extensively. Even if your opponent has only the jack (as in this example), you have lost your ability to maneuver. Prepare to abandon ship.

Of course, a holder of big cards also cringes when the board pairs (unless it makes him a set/full house). But this does not detract from the principle that a board pair hurts the little cards more than it does the big ones.

We haven't mentioned shooting your way out. In this example, you could try the "standard" bluff when the board pairs. You are on the button, just where you wanted to be, just where you were advised to be with the little cards. However, when bluff time comes, the enemy gets the *first shot at it* ... and you cannot call if he bets! Furthermore, if he checks, your bluff bet will be suspect as mere opportunism. He will take you off more often than you will take him. A board pair is a stab in the heart to garbage cards. ♣

# Chapter 17

# The Kill Button

Kill games are very popular in today's poker scene. Like it or not, you probably will be playing with a kill button. A kill button affects garbage play. I have heard players say that kill games are exactly like regular games except that the stakes are higher ... and that the kill structure makes little difference. Wrong!

The meaningful differences are:

(a) With the kill in effect, fewer people will enter the action because some players are intimidated by the bigger bucks.

(b) The person on the kill button tends to play almost every time. Why he does this, I don't know for sure, but it may be because he sees the kill as a challenge that he cannot refuse and still maintain his ego.

Given the second assumption, isolation is injured. You still want to raise — but do so only when you have higher-type cards and good position on the kill button (that is, you are behind it.) A couple of small cards upstream from the kill button are paying too much. ♣

# Chapter 18

# Deception on the Flop

In limit hold'em, the bets double on the turn, and it is best to get the most, or save the most, at that point. To do this, you have the opportunity to play your hand deceptively on the flop for one-half price. In this chapter, we will be examining the very common hold'em practice of playing a hand on the flop in a way that is opposite to its true character. In no-limit hold'em (*real* poker), players use deception wherever they think that it will work best against their opponents. First you get your hand and then you get your man. (Ah, well ... those days are mostly history.)

First, let us pay homage to the truism which says that if there is a lot of money already in the pot, you want to play your hand in a straightforward manner. This is good advice. If the pot is large and you have just flopped two big pair, then you want to bet. Four calls on the flop are worth more than one call on the turn. In this instance, deception is not called for mathematically. Isolation is called for: Giving free cards could kill your hand. This standard advice should be the controlling factor of your action. Therefore, all players will play directly on the flop if the pot is large, right? Wrong.

Curiously, the above truism often is ignored. It seems that deception is a personal thing ... something one does, something that the personality compels or does not compel. Playing deceptively is a personal choice that is done more often by those players who are disposed to do it, without regard to pot odds. In the mind of the actor, deception is the "right" thing to do, the "normal" thing to do. Also note that, since it is the normal thing to do, it is the thing that the actor expects *you* to do to *him!*

This gives rise to two observations: (a) The size of the pot does not affect deception; and (b) Players expect the same as they give. Players who use deception expect you to play similarly. Those who do not use deception are the most susceptible to it when it is dispensed by you.

Rocks wait for the best cards and drive them until someone shows them that they can't win — ho-hum. As a garbage player, you are constantly trying to read the opposition on the flop. The garbage player *needs* a read, a tell, a tiny quick glance of the eye ... a plan. Part of that plan is recalling which opponents like to play their hands *oppositely* on the flop.

All of your opponents can be grouped into two categories. There are those who use deception on the flop, and those who do not try to deceive you on the flop ... two big vats ... two human file drawers, in or out ... she does or she doesn't ... he is or he isn't ... guns or knives.

The plan is simple enough. Each category expects its own in return — so, you will do the opposite. Against the direct-play people, you will be deceptive: Slow play on the flop with a big hand, and bet out or raise when you are on a draw or pressing a small pair. Against the deceptors, you will bet your hand straightforwardly: Bet the bigs and check the draws. Simple, right?

Unfortunately, it just isn't possible to know and categorize every player when casinos have five tables going at your limits or when people are playing with their friends' money; and when players are in and out of the game. However, some shortcuts to evaluate your opponents are available.

**First shortcut.** Use no deception against the "pleasure player." Sometimes you are up against a player who is just out to have a good time, playing his/her hands without paying any attention to what you do or don't do. (You can see this without waiting for a volume of play.) Why use deception if a player is oblivious to you? Against them, forget deception. If you have it, bet it. If you have a draw, check.

**Second Shortcut:** Use deception on the ordinary — and therefore, *good* — player.

**Third Shortcut:** Gambling can be an ethnic thing. There are some cultures, thousands of miles apart, in which gambling has been accepted for thousands of years. A good share of their membership comes to casinos. They love to gamble; their ancestors gambled; it is an expected and honorable thing to do. Sophisticated deception in gambling is normal; it is expected. Play them as deceptors. Of course, playing deceptively is not related to honesty, but rather to the sophisticated concept of deception that is an accepted element in gambling.

Some deceptors love to give you a lot of talk with the deception, while others sit stone silent. Pay no attention to this. The point is that the chips are being bet to the opposite of the hand: A big hand is for limping; a draw is for raising. Against known deceptors, bet your hand *directly* on the flop, and have no fear of multiple raises. If the flush card hits on the turn, try to think of birds and waterfalls ... because you are dead meat!

Interestingly, the talk given with deception is a poor resource for tells. Since deception is allowable, is acceptable, it carries no guilt — thus, there are no altered patterns for our eyes and ears to pick up.

This chapter has focused on flop bets, or their absence, because the flop so often is where deception is used in limit hold'em. Expanding for a moment from flop betting to *any* betting that is opposite to the character of the holding (including all bluffing), we can see a pattern developing for all deceptive betting. This pattern is a part of the levels of play that are described in the next chapter. ♣

# Chapter 19

# Card Reading and Levels of Play

Y ou can't con an honest man because he won't try to get something for nothing. By the same token, you can't get results from deception if your opponent pays no attention to what you might be holding.

**Level One**. This type of opponent operates at level I. He sees what he has — maybe he has made two pair — and says to himself, "I have a good hand." Then he proceeds to bet or call to the very end. Playing at Level I is nothing to be ashamed of: We were all there at one time. Some games have a lot of these types. Treat each one kindly — They may not know much about poker, but they are not stupid. Being rude to them will cause them to go away, and then the entire table will try to find ways to punish you. No good.

Against Level I players, play your cards in a straightforward manner. In essence, you match your level of thought to theirs. You choose to play directly since you know that deception will not work.

**Level Two.** A level two player thinks about (1) what he has; and then (2) compares it with what your hand looks like, what your play is saying. All games have Level 2 players. A rock can exist and survive at this level. Deception works at Level 2. You match your thinking to your Level 2 opponent, and then you choose to play deceptively. He will observe it and, perhaps, be guided by it. You now slow-play your set so as to get two big bets on the turn and one on the river.

**Level Three.** A level three player thinks about (1) what he has; (2) compares it with what your hand figures to be, what your play is saying; and then (3) considers how each of you might be trying to mislead the other. You match your thinking to his at Level 3, and then you probably choose to play directly. Straightforward play works at Level 3, just as it did at Level 1. You now bet your big hand on the flop because your opponent will suspect deception, and may not correctly read your bet as coming from a big hand. If you are on a draw, you check, because your opponent might assume that you are slow-playing. The direct play at Level 3 also is good because your bets are consistent with the basic nature of your hands.

All garbage players are Level 3 players: We have to be to survive! We put our opponents on their levels ... one, two, or three. This categorizing of the enemy is closely related to the categorization that is described in Chapter 18, "Deception on the Flop." In fact, the two are inseparable.

There is no end to levels of play, in the sense that if your opponent expects you to play straightforwardly at Level 3, you then can outdo him by playing deceptively. This then would be Level 4; and if he has figured that out, you would play directly (Level 5), and so on. The fact is that you need only three levels. Some players like to brag about how many levels they are able to think, to which I quietly yawn. Letting ego affect play is not a good idea.

The important thing to remember is that you want to be playing at the same mental level as your opposition. From this position, this firing platform, you can use both deception and direct play — your choice — to outwit the enemy. At Level 1, you choose to play straightforwardly because deception probably is useless. At Level 2, you choose deception. At Level 3, you usually choose direct play; at level 4, deception, and on and on. However, if there were a Level 4, you would just as soon be playing at Level 2 ... because you play your hands the same way at both levels.

In theory, the number of levels at which you might play may go on to infinity. The betting patterns at both Level 8 and Level 2 are the same: deception. Level 1, Level 3, Level 5 and so on call for straightforward play. One could suppose that if you are matching an opponent at Level 98, you would choose deception. But how can you be sure that he isn't at Level 97 or 99? If he is playing at Level 97, then you are playing the wrong strategy. To worry about this is absurd.

For this reason, you need only categorize your opponents into one of the first three levels. If the opposition is at Level 3, play directly. If he is at Level 2, play deceptively. If an opponent picks up on your pattern of play at Level 3, for example, give it about a 10 percent variation and then do something ... do anything ... to make sure that he notices it. I mean, show it ... talk about it. That's all there is to it. Level 3 ends it.

On occasion, you will match wits with a player who puts you on certain levels, so you try to change. You put him on certain levels, so he tries to change. This is akin to a draw in chess: You both are moving up and down without making any headway. Since you are not fixed and neither is your opponent, you have no alternative but to fall back on instinct — based on what you and he did the last time you sparred, the time before that, and his body language. If you *feel* that this is the time for straightforward play, go for it. If you *feel* that deception is the best play, then do it.

Note that this phenomenon is not "levels of play:" It is the *abandonment* of levels. It is like people who cure themselves of an obsessive neurosis. They go out the topside by acquiring so much knowledge about themselves that before long, they realize they didn't need it to begin with. ♣

# Chapter 20

# Seating Position

One topic on which there is too much confusing advice is "seating position at the poker table." Not that all of the advice is bad — It's just that there are so many exceptions that the rules seem to blur away. If this ... if that ... then this ... then that ... and on and on and on.

One small item seems to survive and to be accepted by the poker populace: Have the "action" player sitting somewhere to your right so that his money will come to you as the result of your being seated to his left.

We can do better than that. We can make a *usable* rule. To get there, the thinking goes like this:

(a) The current recommendations are too complicated.

(b) It is correct to have the action to your right.

(c) Hold on! Perhaps it is even better to have the action *directly across* from you. Everyone else at the table wants a piece of Mr. Action. If you are sitting immediately to his left, it hurts. When Mr. Action bets, he drives you into some superior hands. It is expensive to be reraised after getting on the wagon with good, but not great, holdings.

(d) At the very least, you do not want him to be seated on your left because he won't let you steal the pot. And you cannot isolate well because he will call, which will bring in other players ... thus defeating your attempt to isolate.

(e) You live by isolation, the steal raise. That confirms it: You definitely do not want Mr. Action on your left.

(f) I want the opponents in the seats to my left, about the first three seats, to be players who will fold when I raise, or whom I can, at least, manipulate by my actions.

(g) One cannot be perfect in selecting a seat because players move around and change. They also change their betting patterns depending upon whether they are stuck or ahead or mad or happy. Wait a minute! Those rocks ... they always play the same way. *And* they remain in one seat until it is glued to their bottoms.

(h) If the rocks stay glued to one seat, then they should be included in the seating position formula. Besides, I am programmed to kill rocks, and they will throw away when I raise.

So ... here's that usable rule I promised: *Put the rocks to your left* and all else falls into place! So it is. So it is. Amen. ♣

# Chapter 21

# Your Image: Do It!

It is costly to play garbage every hand. The trick is to play it at *selected* times while making the table *think* that you are playing it every hand. Further, you do not want the opposition to be running over your little cards.

Three principles can be used to accomplish these goals:

(a) You want the enemy to think that you play garbage every time. This is the "Little Card" image.

(b) You do not want the enemy to ever think that you have a quality hand. This is the "Not Big-Card" image.

(c) You do not want the enemy to bluff you. This is the "Defensive" image.

## ♣ The Little-Card Image

To make them think that you always hold little cards is important because you can steal pots. What? Yes, it's true! The enemy can never put you on any particular hand. Thus, when you are convinced that nobody has what is out there, you can buy the pot. I constantly am amazed that a known garbage player such as myself, for example, can steal pots with ease, and from multiple opponents. If they thought that I played only the highest two or three cards, it would be impossible for me to steal anything.

Big-card players contend that their playing style is best because when a big card comes, they can steal the pot. We are even better off. When *little* cards come, we can steal ... and we also can steal when a single big card comes. We get the whole deck — The rocks get only the two top cards! You want the enemy to think that you could have *anything* in your hand. "Little-Card" image players can bluff.

## ♣ The Not Big-Card Image

Making them think that you seldom hold big cards is related to the "little-card image," but it is not exactly the same thing. If the enemy thinks that you *never* have big cards, they will give you call after call when you *do* have the top pair. Garbage players get exactly as many quality hands as the rocks ... but garbage players get paid better for them. The "Not Big-Card" image gets calls.

## ♣ The Defensive Image

Little-card players do not want to be bluffed. This requires a defensive image. If you are known as a player who will back down to an overcard, the enemy will soon run over you. This is a bad thing because it puts you to a decision. It will make you decide, each time, whether the opponent has a superior hand. *What you want* is for the enemy to bet *only* when he/she *thinks* that they have the best of it. That way, you can correctly make your move. Being run over is an occupational hazard to the little-card player. If you can convince the opposition that you are likely to defend, then you're way ahead of the game.

A big-card player has only slight need for a defensive image. He survives by having the best cards and driving them home. He doesn't worry about the occasional attack. If the big cards don't hit, he simply dumps his hand and waits for a better time to hunt rabbits with a cannon. On the other hand, a defensive image is a necessity to the small-card player.

We want these three images, but wanting them does not make them happen. The three images — little-card, not big-card, and defensive — must be created deliberately and intentionally. I am happy to defer on this subject to the image sections of John Fox's fine book, *Play Poker, Quit Work, and*

*Sleep Till Noon.* Get this book and read the chapters on image. (I wonder if his real name is Fox? Seems appropriate enough ...)

Here are a few rules as my examples. Before you read them, make some peace with yourself about how much you are willing to lie in a poker game. Some lying always is ethical; some lying always is unethical. It is always ethical to see a flop and then exclaim that you have a hand that you do not have. It is always ethical to muck a hand and announce a false holding to the table in general. It is always unethical to lie about whether you have looked at your cards. I do not lie if a friend directly asks about what I just held. If I prefer privacy, I say that I will tell him in the bar. This saying is accepted by both the player and the rest of the table, and you should develop your own. Now for some examples of image play.

## ♣ Examples of Image Play

(1) **Show little cards.** When you play small cards, privately show them before the flop to a player at your side who is not in the pot. (Of course, do not do this in tournaments.) (Little-Card image)

(2) **Don't show big cards.** An example of how *not* to do it is this: I once showed a Q-J to a neighbor, flopped an open set, and later had to make a "good" laydown. My neighbor went off like a newscaster for 10 minutes. My defensive image was injured in the eyes of my opponents. Some of them remembered my play, and I had no one to blame but myself. (Not Big-Card image)

(3) **Always exaggerate on the flop** so that it appears that you never really have much in comparison to your declaration. For example, "Hey, I flopped quads again!" Jacks-up doesn't look like much now. (Not Big-Card image)

(4) **When you open a high-card hand,** do it quietly and without display tactics. To win, you have to show the hand ...

but keep your mouth shut while you're doing it. (Not Big-Card image)

(5) **When you muck a high-card hand**, do it without comment. Also, lie about it, as explained below. (Not Big-Card image)

(6) **As you muck** pocket queens, announce, "A 7-5 just can't get it *every* time," or "I'm sick of *always* calling with third-best." (Little-Card and Defensive image)

(7) **While giving a call,** make a little display: "I call it," or "I'll see you just *one more* time," or "Take that bluff and stick it!" (Defensive and Little-Card image)

(8) **When you win with garbage,** make a display of it. Maybe announce that, "I had it all the time!" or "How could anybody be stuck at *this* table?" (Defensive and Little-Card image)

(9) **Before you muck garbage,** pick it up so that your out-of-the-pot neighbors might see it. Don't worry: They *will* look! (Little-Card image) If you are lucky, some dolt will make you show the hand to the whole table. Do this pickup in front of yourself; that is, not in the manner of a sneak show to a friend at your side.

(10) **When you lose with garbage,** lay it open and say, "I misread my hand because I looked at the same seven twice," or "Why do I always put you on a flush draw?" (Little-Card and Defensive image)

(11) **It is helpful to be known as a player who bluffs,** and a good way to get that recognition is to talk about doing it. Sometimes I say, "Just because I bluff a lot doesn't mean that I have a hand now and then." Mentally, the opposition wants to correct your logic, but must first buy into your premise to do so. They will do this, even though they say nothing. You have hooked them.

(12) through (?) **You write these.** That's right — Write them in advance, plan them, and act them out. Your image does not just happen; you must work on it. My sayings may

not be right for you. Break it down to the three principles that I mentioned earlier and plan 10 sayings for each principle. Make them things that *you* would say. Don't be shy now.

There are opposites to the proper image creation. Just for fun, here is a sample list of how *not* to do it ... how to make it even *harder* to win the next pot. These are ways to prove that you play *only* big cards, never play little ones, and *can* be run over. I call it "The Sheriff's Garden of Image Horrors." (They call me "The Sheriff" because I don't let anybody steal a pot ... I really don't.)

## ♣ The Sheriff's Garden of Image Horrors

Remember: This is how *not* to do it ...

(1) **Being beaten.** You have just had your pocket queens or your A-K suited beaten by an 8-4 offsuit. Show your cards to the table and say, "Damn dealer! That's the third big pocket pair she's busted in the last 10 minutes!"

(2) **Being right.** You open for a raise and are reraised twice by the time it gets back to you. You show your A-Q to prove how well you started *and* to prove how you are capable of making a good laydown. You now can win the election as the tightest player at the table. Well, just try and eat that!

(3) **Complaining.** "I've just lost $400 without winning a single pot, and every time, I've had a big pair or A-K. Change the %$#@!! deck!"

(4) **Disgust throw.** You don't play your blind, and then make a disgusted face and burn your cards into the muck, displaying to all that you are *entitled* to big cards and are waiting for them.

(5) **Quiet fold with small cards.** You put in a call on your big blind with small cards and later need to fold. Quietly, you slip your hand into the muck so that nobody will ever accuse you of bad play. Your chances of winning the table election as

best player is intact: You are the right person ... you are the *most* right person in the world!

(6) **The player showed his (big) hand.** It was the first hand of a small, no-limit tournament and as a couple of players mucked their hands, the next player asked, "Is this no-limit?" Then he made a remark about how he wouldn't have sat down if he had known. This was believable; he was frustrated. The next hand, a player made a small bet and our man went all in. He was not called. The game was on! Then ... then ... *then* the player showed his two kings before he threw them in. The valuable image that he had created, that of a wild dunce, was dashed. In 30 seconds, he had created an image that I need a week to create — instant donkey — and then he threw it all away for nothing.

(7) **The blind waiter.** There is a small advantage to a new player letting the blind go by and then posting the same amount in good position. On average, let's say that this move is worth two chips. What does the table think when a player sits down two seats in front of the blinds, announces that he will wait, and smirks at his opponents for five hands while he waits to post his blind? Without ever playing a hand, this moron has proven that he is patient, and that he will play only when he thinks he has an advantage. Who does he think will give him action ... Santa? He has just kissed off 20 chips in calls during the next hour. If you must come in from behind, pretend to choke on some food, yell, walk off to see an imaginary friend — do something, do *anything*, but don't sit and smirk.

Watch for the players around you to prove that they play big cards, *only* big cards, and are willing to lay down a good hand. You will know how much they're giving away. What is more, you will have a fine grip on how to play those same players five minutes later. ♣

# Chapter 22

# The Maniac and
# The Little Cards

The maniac gives action and plenty of it — the kami-kaze draws, the bets in the dark, the cap with an A-5 offsuit. We love it. Really? *Really?* Well, maybe not. We little-card players are programmed to kill rocks. The maniacs are programmed to kill us!

Garbage players have great difficulty in "good" games. With action comes danger for a little-card player. Specifically, our standard deviation goes through the roof; our status as isolationist leader follows; and we are left with a lot of chips in the pot trying to beat unknown cards that are at least as good as our own. Tough spot.

In Chapter 14, "Drive At Suited Flops," I described flush-draw players and some little things that we can do to counter them; specifically, lead into suited flops and don't fall for an opponent's bet when the third suited card comes to the board. Our adjustment to the flush player comes from our read on him, and we take comfort in our reads. His actions are driven by greed and, therefore, we can understand him.

But the maniac (or his subspecies, the drunk) gives no such clues with his actions. When he has a hunch about a hand, he puts in multiple raises, no matter what kind of hand it is. The board gives us no clue as to his holding. He has no guilt, so his bluffs look the same as though he had the nuts. He has no greed, so we cannot detect deception. To make things worse, it is the maniac who sets the tone of the table; that is, his action is what everybody else keys on. There is likely to be a lot of raising both in front of and behind his seating position. What to do? What to do? *What to do?*

It is big-picture time. There is no "right" way to play poker. For every style of play, there is an opposing style that will defeat it. As the saying goes, "There is a paddle for every bottom." We flex so as to beat the opponent at hand.

### ♣ The "Scissors, Rock, Paper" of Poker

Do you recall the childhood game of scissors, rock, and paper, in which each choice beat the next one in a circle? The same thing is true in poker, and it goes like this:

(1) The rocks beat the maniacs.
(2) The maniacs beat the aggressives.
(3) The aggressives beat the rocks.

We are aggressive; therefore, we beat the rocks. In turn, we are beaten by the maniacs, who are beaten by the rocks. (If you like, you can substitute the words "tight," "loose," and "superloose.") This circle of dominance has long been recognized by insightful players.

The "maniac factor" is the reason why garbage players fare poorly in "good" games. When you are looking for a table to play at, don't be attracted by capped pots. Seek instead a table where a lot of people are entering the pot, but where they also are folding when faced with raises. If you find yourself in a "good" game with lots of raises, you had better adjust to it by changing the hands that you play.

If only one true maniac is in the game, try to sit in opposition to his chair. That way, you won't be betting the pot for him, and his bets won't drag you through the mud. If there are two maniacs in the game, then it is you who must change.

If it is true (and it is) that the maniac beats the aggressive player, then we little-card players are in trouble. The reason is easily explained: To be a little-card player is to be an isolator, an aggressive player. If you can't isolate, you have no viable tool. Maniacs do not discard when we try to isolate: They simply reraise us. The deduction is sad but clear: We must become rocks. Ugly.

When you play against a maniac, stop playing little cards.
When you play against a maniac, stop playing little cards.
When you play against a maniac, stop play ..... ♣

# Chapter 23

# Tournament Strategy

*Editor's Note: D. R. Sherer is a highly respected tournament player who has placed in the money at the Queens Classic, World Series of Poker, Commerce Club, and Bicycle Club. In January, 1996, he was listed in sixth place in Poker World magazine's compilation of top money winners in no-limit hold'em tournaments for the previous six months (net winnings: $49,516). Prior to that, a national rating service ranked Sherer as third in the world for no-limit hold'em tournaments with a buy-in of $1,000-$2,500. Of the 12 major tournaments that he entered in 1994, Sherer reached the final table six times and shared first-place money twice.*

If garbage players win tournaments, then a chapter on how to win them belongs in this book. In this section, I discuss seven areas of tournament strategy that differ from money-game strategy. First, the "speed" of a tournament.

## ♣ Tournament Speed

The two elements that determine the speed of a tournament are (a) The size of your original stack in relation to the size of the starting big blind; and (b) The frequency with which the size of allowable bets increases. The faster a tournament moves, the less skill has to do with who wins. We like *slow.*

If the original stack size is small, then action begins quickly. If the increases in bet-amount come quickly (say, every 20 minutes), then all action is just short of being desperate. Theoretically, the size of the increases in bet-amount could come into play, but most tournaments make the rises about double, or just less than that, for each round (20 minutes, 30 minutes, one hour, and so on) in a tournament. The size of your original stack has an impact on the initial speed of the tournament. After a while, the rises catch up to the size of your initial stack. When the slowing effect of the buy-in stack is gone, it does not return. The only remaining speed-maker is the length of the round (the time of play at each betting level).

**Slow-Fast-Slow-Fast.** A "mature" tournament with full life has a pattern all its own. That pattern is slow-fast-slow-fast. Let me explain: The tournament can start with an adequate issue of chips; say, the chip issue is 200 times the big blind ... a slow time. After a few rises in bet-amount, players begin going out. At this point, there are many short stacks and desperate play occurs ... a fast time. *Fast* continues through a few more rounds until all of the chips are concentrated in the stacks of fewer players.

The second slow period comes when, for example, about six tables are left out of 20. Many stacks are large. Players become quiet and deadly serious. At the final table, the rises again force fast action, usually beginning at about six-handed play and continuing to heads-up. At six-handed, the fact that three players have been eliminated from the final table is an indication that the rises are holding sway and "fast is back."

From this description, you can see the slow-fast-slow-fast pattern of a tournament:

(1) Buy-in, slow.

(2) Middle, fast.

(3) Late middle, slow.

(4) Final, fast.

Some tournaments (to my mind, all *real* tournaments) start with enough chips so that the size of the big blind is not a threat to your starting stack. You can play tight if you wish, and most players do just that. Not many players bust out in this initial round. It is a slow time.

**Playing Against Maniacs.** Nevertheless, there is a little kicker during this first slow period: the maniac. These dolts (in limit hold'em tourneys, they are dolts; in no-limit tournaments, they are not) have read some place that it is good to take chances in order to build up chips early. They translate this advice into absurd play.

Since it is a slow period, you should be able to steal with small cards. However, if one of these fast maniacs is inserted into your table, you must quickly identify him and play *only* big cards whenever it appears that he will be playing in the pot. Small cards are in jeopardy during the first slow period because of the presence of maniacs.

By the time the second slow period rolls around, most of the maniacs either have been eliminated or have become so impressed with their big pile of chips that they have stopped playing wildly and have begun to try to preserve their chips. This makes for a great time to steal.

**Structure and Pattern.** The structure of a tournament determines its pattern. A typical rebuy event has no slow start. You start fast, and after the break, you start fast again. The pattern is fast-slow-fast. In almost any tournament that starts with short stacks, the first slow period is eliminated. A one-table satellite is a good example: The action is fast-slow-fast, and the *slow* is almost imperceptible.

Any tournament can be structured to be fast, of course. But it is the amount of *slow* that allows a player's skill to be maximized. The best example of a tournament that empha-sizes the skill factor is the *World Series of Poker* at Binion's Horseshoe. It has two-hour rounds at each betting level. The buy-in gives you $10,000 in chips with a big-blind of $50. Since the starting stack is 200 times the big blind, we can rate the start at 200. A small sample of tournaments is listed here so that you can get a feel for this rating factor. (Tournament structures change from time to time, so read this list for thought purposes only.)

| Start Rate | Rounds | Tournament |
|:---:|:---:|:---|
| 200 | 2 hours | Binion's Horseshoe World Series of Poker, $10,000 Championship |
| 200 | 1 hour | Oceanside Casino Seniors World Championship $2,000 Championship Event |
| 100 | 1 hour | Bicycle Club $5,000 Championship Event |
| 100 | 45 mins | Oceanside Casino $300 tournament |
| 50 | 40 mins | Commerce Club $500 No-limit Hold'em |
| 30 | 1 hour | Foxwoods World Finals Hold'em Tournament |
| 33 | 45 mins | Commerce Club $300 Limit Hold'em |
| 33 | 40 mins | Bicycle Club $500 No-limit Hold'em |
| 25 | 40 mins | Commerce Club $300 No-limit Hold'em |
| 30 | 20 mins | Bicycle Club $20 evening tournaments |
| 20 | 15 mins | Standard for Satellites |
| 20 | 15 mins | Hollywood Park $20 evening tournaments |

I believe that all tournament advertisements should state three important details: number of starting chips, starting blinds, and length of rounds. It leaves a poor taste in my mouth when I travel to a tournament only to find that its structure favors "getting lucky," that almost everyone busts out early, and that the management prides itself on how fast it can move tournament players into the room's ring games. I suggest that you call every tournament director in advance to obtain full information for each scheduled event. Why would you want to travel even 10 miles without knowing the tournament's structure?

Promotional tournaments usually are very fast. To enter these in-house promotions, you usually must play x-number of hours to qualify for the tournament, in which you can win a car, a vacation, or thousands of dollars. I have found it painful to put in the effort to qualify only to find that the tournament structure is so fast that the winner's name may as well have been drawn from a bin. I suggest asking the tournament director for a structure sheet of the final tournament before you spend a lot of time qualifying for these promotionals.

How about playing the supersatellites and the minisatellites? Thousands in return for a small entry fee! If you like *fast*, these satellites offer the ultimate in speed, since you start with so few chips and the blinds rise very quickly. *Slow* comes only a short time before the final table action begins.

Hands such as 7♣ 6♣ have no real chance during all those prolonged fast periods in satellites. It cannot find a big-stack customer when it hits; it costs dear chips from your short stack when it misses; and some desperado will usually move in on your opening bet, leaving you no room to maneuver.

For this discussion, supersatellites are the province of the big cards. Doubly bad for a small-card player is that his skills at playing shorthanded are counterfeited. At the final table, you must stop playing in order to survive long enough to capture one of the seats in the big tournament. (Tom McEvoy reminds us in *Tournament Poker* that your goal in a supersatellite is *not* to win it; your goal is to *place high* enough to win a seat in the big tournament.) Usually, three to five seats will be awarded, eliminating your shorthanded skills.

I have a friend with a great deal of tournament experience; the only weakness he has (in my opinion) is that he waits for big cards. He does well in supersatellites. If you play one,

I recommend his style. As when playing against maniacs, the garbage player must be able to leave his best game at home. If you can't do that, when why waste your money? Get into a one-table satellite instead. "Hold on!" you argue, "The one-tables are also a fast place." True, one-table satellites are fast, but they have one great feature in favor of the garbage player: They become shorthanded right away. You don't have to wait for hours — it is instant final table.

A standard one-table satellite starts fast and gets faster. At the four-handed or five-handed point, there may be a time when chips concentrate, but that moment passes quickly. By the time it gets to three-handed action, things are in overdrive again. No player is replaced. Making deals is infrequent, so the satellite progresses to heads-up play. As a garbage player, you *know* imperfect starts and how to get value for them. This makes you a big favorite.

The trick is for you to lay low until the first four players are busted out, which usually means at least three betting levels or about 45 minutes to an hour. During this time, you must play very carefully, keeping your aggression in check. After that, you are a big overlay. Another factor that demands tight play early is the presence of one or two maniac types. You must keep a low profile until their terror ends. They are good candidates for the first four bustouts; but while they still are in action, avoid them like the plague. If the maniac survives for the first hour or so, then still try to avoid him. Hopefully, he is seated to your right — You may be able to anticipate his presence and obtain a seat to his left.

A garbage player belongs in one-table satellites, not in the supers and minis. Of course, the big tournament itself is our natural habitat. Those hours of juicy, slow rounds, capped by playing shorthanded, are our finest moments. Try not to shoot off all your money in the supers.

## ♣ The Curve

In the beginning, everything is equal. But as players are eliminated and other players are transferred from broken tables, the stacks at your table *do not* fairly represent "average" stacks. It is always helpful to know where your stack stands in relation to the size of the average stack in the room, the "median" stack. As an example, suppose that a tournament starts with 100 players who each are given $1,000 in chips. An hour later, a player at your table has 5,000 chips and you are down to 850. You think that you're behind, and you feel a little desperate. However, if there still are 90 players in the tournament, your stack is not much shorter than the average stack. You are behind the curve, but only by a small amount. You need not feel desperate, and can wait. You can ignore the 5,000-chip stack because it is an aberration. Concentrate on finding sound moves.

The same thing helps when you are ahead. Suppose that you have 2,000 chips against the 5,000-unit stack. You want to be leading, like he is. You want to play to gain equal power. Hold it! You have doubled up; you are at "double the curve." That 5,000 stack is not ahead of you. You and he are co-leaders, together with many others. Relax and look for solid opportunities.

If you are well ahead of the curve, you can slow down a little and just play heavy cards. If you are well behind the curve, it may be best for you to look for ways to double up. I say "look for ways to double up," but I do not (repeat, *do not*) suggest going out in a blaze of glory. Your small stack is valuable: Don't give up. Find a good investment for it, and with a bit of luck, you will be returned to your rightful position of dominance with enough chips to bully the other stacks.

Determining the curve does not require exact math; an estimate will be adequate. Rough numbers will do just fine because what you want is a general understanding of your *relationship* to the curve: Are you at it, double it, one-half of it, or where? If the tournament started with 35 tables and 17 of them are still in action, then the average stack should be double the size of the beginning number of chips. (Say you started with 1,000 chips: The average stack would now number 2,000 chips.) Naturally, this gets complicated because of rebuys and unsold seats, but you can overcome these factors.

We would like to know the size of the *median* stack, rather than the *mean*. That is, we want to know the size of the middle player's stack. The median is better because it more fairly compares your stack with those of the other players. The downside limit in a tournament is the loss of all your chips; there is no corresponding upper limit. As players go down, they go out; but the leaders can have stacks that are several times the average. Thus, the median will be slightly lower than the mean. We cannot easily calculate the median, so the plan is to determine the mean and then estimate the curve at a somewhat lower number.

To get the mean, you can count tables for a while, and then later, count players. In the early stage, you know what the average player has because almost all players are still in action. At the first break, the number of players and rebuys are always posted. From this you can calculate the average stack per player and make a small pocket note. See how many players are left, and then figure the average stack. For example, if the average stack for each starting player is 1,250 (100 players and 150 rebuys each for 500 chips), and if there are 40 players still in the tournament, the *mean* stack is 3,125. Suppose you have about 6,000 chips. Your stack size is double the curve — You can relax and catch bandits. Or suppose you are right about *at* the curve with 3,075 chips — You have a good reason to *not* panic, to not do desperate deeds. But what if you are at one-third of the curve (around 1,000 chips)? You'd better start looking for opportunities to make a move.

A running feel for the curve will give you *control* over your decisions. It is the most important factor in determining the style of play that you choose for the moment.

## ♣ Short Chips

There are two times when being short on chips becomes a factor in a tournament. One is when *you* have the problem, and the second is when the entire room has it.

If the tournament start is fast, you may be ahead of the curve, say, one hour into it, and find yourself in a situation in which all the players still have small stacks — the whole room is short on chips. Under these conditions, you cannot play small cards. The clearest example of such a scenario is the large supersatellite right after the break. Players have made their rebuys and add-ons, which can give them a false feeling of "I've got plenty of chips." The catch is that the blinds have just gone up so much that every player in the room is desperate for chips. To come barging into a pot with small cards is suicide. Although your strategy still is to bring it in for a raise, you can only do that with larger cards. Why? Because you very likely will get a response of all-in by a short stack. You cannot fold players or get implied odds on a call. A bring-in with small cards, be it a call or a raise, is just an invitation to action that you do not want before the flop.

If the desperadoes are on your immediate left, the problem is even worse. Unless the "purchase" move with a small pair is all-in, or close to it, you are not likely to get the odds that you need to justify playing the small pair. And, you do not want to pay several more bets just to see if your small pair can survive on its own. The purchase move with the small connectors is bad, and hits are not properly paid. Therefore, play only the bigs during these fast times.

The opposite of *room fast* is *room slow*. *Room slow* is the time for the steal bring-in. The steal bring-in is vital in tournaments. Once most of the room is comfortable with the size of the blinds, and the players to your left are too, then the chances of a desperate move from one of them is small. You are free to make the steal move with smaller-type cards. (More about this in "Steal Raise Occasions" a couple of sections later.)

Being on personal shorts (having a short stack) is a different matter. In a fine *Card Player* magazine article written by Michael Cappelletti, he instructs that if you have 10 or more big bets left in your stack, you can slow down and play heavy cards. If you have three to nine big bets left, be careful, but venture to win chips. If you have two or fewer big bets, look for two reasonable cards and put in your chips. This is good advice: It even works for no-limit tournaments. Simply calculate a big bet as being the size of two big blinds and divide that number into the size of your stack. Even when the entire room is short, your short chips may require a move with something less than the bigs. I will describe this play in more detail in the section that follows on "Garbage Versus Desperation."

In sum, your approach to playable hands in a tournament is affected by three variables:

(1) Your stack size in relation to the average stack, or where you are on the curve;

(2) Your stack in relation to the big blind, or personal speed; and,

(3) The room-in-general's stack size in relation to the big blind, or general speed.

Number one guides us on overall aggressiveness and approach. Numbers two and three guide us on starting hand requirements, calling hands, and steal potential.

## ♣ Garbage versus Desperation

What happens when you are short on chips during a fast period in the tournament? As I discussed in the previous section, the small cards do *not* want to face desperate players, but you can't always choose when to be short. In fact, it is more likely that your desperate moments will come during the fast parts of the tournament. Then what do you play? The left column below contains hands that might be playable during desperation time. The right column lists hands that are not playable when you are desperate. You would rather kiss a mountain lion than play the second column against desperadoes.

| Do Play These | Don't Play These |
|:---:|:---:|
| A♣ 3♥ | 9♦ 6♦ |
| Q♦ 8♣ | 8♥ 7♣ |
| J♣ 9♥ | 5♥ 4♥ |
| 10♦ 8♣ | J♣ 2♣ |
| K♦ 6♠ | 6♠ 5♠ |

All too often I see a player make a move with cards like those in the second column and get sent out the door by someone with one king or one 10. Being suited or connected is insignificant compared to whether your high card strength will be enough to survive. During fast times, all choices are related to the bigness of your cards against desperadoes.

During the fast periods in a tournament, how big is *big*? The answer to this question is complicated by the nagging and ever-present trade-off between playing one large card or two medium ones. Would you rather have K-2 or J-9? The high card is the first item of choice, so long as it is an ace and, to some extent, a king. From the rank of queen on down, you look at the size of the two cards as a whole. Note the Q-8 and the J-9 in the above "Do Play" column: The eight is big enough to be a good companion, whereas a six, and certainly a five, usually would not be big enough. The seven does not fit, either. Halfway up the stairs is a stair where I sit, and the seven sits with me. In desperate situations, try not to be dealt a seven!

All of the hands in the second column are just about equally poor. Wait for something that is bigger than the texture of the hands represented in the right column ... it's easy to do. As a matter of fact, it is a little difficult to have hands as bad as those in the second column. Deal out a deck and see how many hands have an ace, a king, or two cards higher than a seven. Close to one-half of the hands will pass this test.

Playable hands that start with a queen, jack, 10, or nine all are connected — This is a coincidence! Do *not* confuse their connected appearance with the *real* reason for playing them: You play them for their overall bigness. Inexperienced players ignore good hands, and then give undue weight to the connected or suited nature of smaller ones. They get a trip to valet parking for their mistake.

## ♣ Limp Occasions

Tournaments give me an opportunity to limp. Some tournament players really work at being a big shark in a little puddle. They constantly run over the table. They do it deliberately and they plan it in advance. Their thinking is that they can muscle more chips into their stacks than go out to anyone with the nuts. They win big or they lose big. And since the real money is paid to only a few, winning big will get the job done. After all, if you are out, you are out. It makes no difference if you bet it up or were slowly ground down. They have a point.

We adjust. I have had success by limping in with a quality hand out of position, and letting the shark try to bully me all the way to the river. This character has a Jeckel and Hyde personality. In ring games, he plays more cautiously. In tournaments, the Hyde comes out. (Or would it be a goldfish and shark personality?) Use him.

Akin to the sharks are the desperadoes, the short-stack players who watch the opener for a clue — any clue will do — that tells them to make a move at the pot. They expect a raise from big cards. After all, the books say to raise with two big cards, right? Your limp represents a weak play to them, probably small connectors. When you limp in, the desperadoes dive in with small and insane holdings. With a little bit of help from the deck, you have them trapped.

If either two desperadoes or one certified shark is at my table, I make a point of limping in out of position with good cards. Sometimes, this can be carried a bit further, by calling a player who opened with a limp. The more players, the more "mechanically" incorrect this maneuver becomes. I suggest that you limit the limp-call to no-limit tournaments, and to those times when there is only one other limper in the pot. If two come in, then play your hand straightforwardly.

I am speaking of limping in out-of-position. Raise as the dealer button gets closer to you. Isolation against the big blind is an immutable tournament law.

No-limit play is different. You may join an unlimited number of limpers so long as the shark is yet to act and is in a feeding frenzy.

## ♣ The Out-of-Position Baby Paint Pairs

The out-of-position medium pairs — Q-Q, J-J, and 10-10 — are tournament trouble. If your stack is very small, you can commit with these hands and cross your fingers. If your stack is very large, you can limp in and hope to drive a set into some other big stack. Unfortunately, I always seem to be holding the medium pairs when my stack is less than bullet-proof. Those of you with tournament experience know the creepy feeling at the back of your neck when you squeeze out these three specific hands.

Say that you have a 10-big-bet stack in an early position of a mostly-full table, and you pick up one of these three pairs. As I discussed in the chapter on "Baby Paints," a pair smaller than these is somewhat protected by its smallness; a pair larger than these is somewhat protected by its largeness. These three are naked on roller skates.

To play them, you may have exactly two options. You may limp in with them out of position, try for a cheap flop, and avoid commitment. Or, you may raise, and by isolating, get full value. Tough choice. You make trouble for yourself *either* way. Let's take a look at that trouble.

**The Trouble with Baby Paint Pairs.** The raise tends to commit you, which is bad. The limp traps desperadoes, which is good. The desperado may have one ace or one king, which is bad. The limp allows you to avoid overcards, which is good. The limp allows one overcard to kill you, which is bad. The limp allows draws and unknown "smalls" into the pot, which is bad. The raise signals out-of-position power to educate the table, which is bad. The limp is deception, which is good. The limp means that you get little information from a raiser, which is bad. And on and on.

Better tournament players than you or I have hit the door with these three hands. In bad position, they *cannot* be played correctly in limit hold'em tournaments and are, therefore, a threat to your immediate survival. A *what*? In a tournament, what could be worse than a threat to your immediate survival? Bad food service, maybe?

Go for the third option, Plan C: Waste them! Muck them! Try the next hand. Visualize them right now, and imagine pitching them. When nobody is looking, get a deck and practice throwing them away just to see how your wrist feels doing it. At the real table, drop one on the floor, lay the other one face up, and say, "This will be the third time I've lost a tournament for doing that." Take the same chips that you would have invested in these middle pairs, and use them to steal a pot.

Pass and think cool thoughts. *No vale la pena.* You may be starving in the woods, but you don't use a .22 to shoot the bear.

In position? Well, that's different ...

## ♣ Steal Occasions

It is not *desirable* that you steal blinds to win a tournament — It is *essential* that you steal blinds to win a tournament. This concept comes to full fruition at the final table as the game gets short. Many times, in four-handed play at the final table, I have seen one of the two players who are in a good position raise the pot, after which the others discard. I mean not just once, but for 10 or 12 hands in a row there was no flop!

(Note: A couple of successful no-limit tournament players that I know don't steal blinds. They let you try it, give you a tiny reraise, and then they try to steal it from you on the flop. The category is the same ... except that they win in big chunks.)

The steal phenomenon flows from that final table down to all betting levels. The holding with which you make the steal is governed by the stack and speed considerations that I previously discussed. What seats are eligible for a steal move? Ah, that makes a difference. The move can be made earlier than the last two seats. Because of the strong reluctance to challenge the move, players are willing to let you isolate more often. The dealer spot plus three seats in front of it are about the maximum positions from which you can try a steal. That is, at a full table, the first two or three seats have trouble trying a steal because there simply are too many possible playing hands behind them ... a mechanical, not a psychological thing.

Catching stealers counts, too. You are not the inventor of the "purchase order." Sometimes, you just know that a particular player is pounding your blind. It will not do to raise him back out of position with junk cards. He knows what he is doing to you, and will not respect your transparent tantrum. He knows that he has been disturbing you and will scoff at your overbet; he is prepared for it. He also is ready to receive the intelligence information that a legitimate raise will convey, and is prepared to look for the difference between a legitimate raise and your frustration jab. Some experts agree that the way to take care of someone who is on your back is to come back at him. I suggest that this does not have to happen in the same betting round.

Here is a play that you really can use: (a) Think for a moment (an act, of course, because you have random garbage); (b) Put in a careful call; (c) On the flop, bet out, no matter what you hold. Sometimes you win, and sometimes you get played with. Take the wins and do the best you can with the action. This is the play that your antagonist did not want to see. You have shown that you will defend *and* you have taken the action from him for the same amount of chips that you would have used by raising. You will be chips ahead ... and he will be off your back.

Now, back to stealing. A lot of players deliberately make a spectacle of themselves with loud talk, wisecrack jokes, and general conduct that attracts attention to themselves. We know them well. They use this conduct to get extra calls. Players may be irritated or otherwise induced to call because of the show-off's act. Now, if *you* are trying to steal, the opposite scenario should hold true ... and it does. To get those steals, you should be, for the most part, the strong and silent type.

At one time, I thought that it was a good idea to steal a pot or two just before the limits rose. My thinking was that the chips were cheaper then, and the play would either win or would inexpensively project a wild image (which I would use a few minutes later at the higher limit). However, I since have done a complete reversal on this idea, and now believe that a steal or two should be done just *after* the limits increase. There are two reasons for this notion. First, the late period steals did not work well, since players tended to make the cheap call. Second, the players tend to be very tight after the limits rise. They act frozen. It seems that the increase scares them, because their stacks have fewer disposable chips. Steals work better just after the limits rise. Try it.

The overall best time to steal is during the second slow period, the *real slow.* After the first break, players start popping out of the tournament. The staff can't break tables fast enough. Players and dealers shout about empty seats, and players with chips in their hands mill around looking for their new tables. This is a *fast time,* so you will not steal.

As chips concentrate into fewer stacks, there are fewer eliminations. Things slowly become very quiet. Stacks are large and players become deadly serious with new-found power. Each one begins to believe that he can win the tournament. You can *hear* the silence. It is like listening for the right time to take popcorn off the heat. One-half of the floormen take their breaks.

As soon as the *second slow,* the serious quiet, you should start pounding on the big blind. *Just don't look at him!*

## ♣ Rebuys

Some tournaments offer a rebuy that you cannot refuse, many more chips for the same price as your buy-in. I look at these rebuys negatively, as it *feels* to me like they are designed to get more money from the players.

It has been established that a true rebuy is correct, because the money that it costs is smaller in proportion to the paid-in pool. That is, if you are out of chips, it usually is correct to rebuy. However, many players expand this concept to incorrectly rebuy when they still have some chips left. A simple but workable rule is that you do not rebuy if you cannot at least double your stack. The tournament doesn't really begin until the add-ons are over. Shane Smith's book on low-limit rebuy tournaments, *Poker Tournament Tips from the Pros*, further explains rebuy philosophies and strategies in the section titled "Rebuying and Adding On." ♣

# Chapter 24

# "Minimum" Starts

All those other fine hold'em books include minimum start proposals. For what it's worth, here is a creation of mine. Just for the record, don't expect me to be following my own advice if you see me across the table in the next game you play.

The numbering system on this chart is correct. It's sort of like all those years before they got the lanes correctly numbered on police reports. Player One is the big blind. Player Two is the little blind. Player Three is the dealer, and Player Four is to the dealer's right. All other seats progress in order up to the number of players in the ring.

**Guidelines for Using the "Minimum" Start Calculations.** Here are some guidelines for using this chart:

(1) Rule one: These holdings are to be used for reference only. Play whatever you think is the best psychological move available to you in your game.

(2) Rule two: Minimum hand requirements are great when you are stuck. They prevent you from rationalizing your poor starts. At these times, I use them myself to keep my play in check.

# "Minimum" Starts

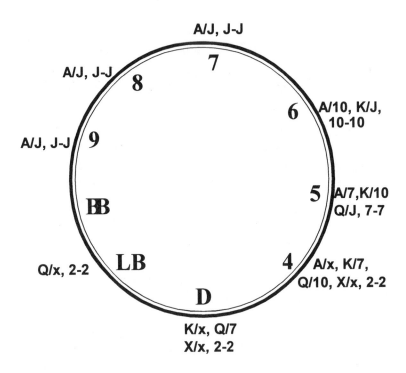

(3) Seats nine, eight, and seven require an ace with either a king, queen, or jack for a kicker.

(4) All hands are brought in for a raise, except the No Fold'em Package discussed in (5) following.

(5) The no-fold'em package of smaller pairs and the A-x and K-x suited must be added to your starts in many games. Limp

in with them unless their high-card value, as shown on the chart, calls for a raise. The high-card value controls your play; limping in with these suited cards is secondary to that consideration. The "suited limp" provides cover for the "small pair limp."

(6) Being suited adds value, but not enough to change the chart. This advice is the opposite of what some people have advised. For instance, in my opinion, a first-position bring in with a suited K-10 or Q-10 is abhorrent, yet it has been recommended as a first-position bring-in on one of the starting hands charts that I have seen. K-Q suited is not, repeat *not,* a quality hand: It is just a K-Q that is worth less than an A-J. It should not be played until the first three players have thrown away, unless you play it as a "no-fold'em limp."

(7) The X/x printed for starts in Seats "D" and Four represent anything that you think will steal the blinds. There simply are no cookbook minimum starts for these two seats.

(8) Others have advised that if you enter a pot after another player already has entered, you need a hand that is as good as an opening hand should be when it is played from an opening position. I disagree. Who says that our opener is going to come into the action correctly? I recommend that you enter the pot when your hand has the expectation of beating the players in it. Period!

*Do not read this paragraph:* OK, if you must, here it is — This chart is a *creation.* Its calculation begins with the cards that are necessary to raise two-handed. Then it works backward to the lowest out-of-position hand that is playable, the A-J. Note that the K-Q is not listed as a playable hand until Seat 6.

Respect is given to the weakness of the two, three, four, five, and six. Respect is given the big differences in value between a king and a queen, and between a queen and a jack insofar as their likelihood of being the top pair on the flop. Respect also is given to the trade-off between having a single high card and having two medium cards of a potential winning rank.

The same method was used for the pairs, starting with two-handed play and working backward to the lowest out-of-position pair that is playable, the J-J. For the purposes of this chart, psychological factors are ignored. It is a mechanical creation. ♣

# Chapter 25

# Norepinephrine, Anyone?

There is no connection between smoking and cards ... or is there? There is no connection between alcohol and cards ... or is there? Cards are not drugs. Why, then, is the treatment for drug addictions so similar to the treatment for compulsive gambling? Here is a connection (my opinion only, of course).

A chemical, a drug, a natural substance, a hormone known as norepinephrine is produced in the brain. It is a neurotransmitter that facilitates the flow of electrons between the neurons of brain cells. Norepinephrine is produced in what is called the "fight-or-flight" situation. That means that the drug is produced automatically when you are in danger, or perhaps when someone close to you is in danger. When it is produced, you can see more, fight harder, run faster, lift more, and jump higher. It is one reason that heroes can do more than the average person. Have a knife pointed at your belly and you will produce some norepinephrine pronto.

It is well known that some soldiers get hooked on combat and must be ordered out of the forward areas. If left to their own desires, these men would choose to stay where life is at risk. We might say that this choice is not logical. Why, then, do they do it? The soldier becomes hooked on his own self-produced norepinephrine and being in risky action gives him a high. He wants it. He needs it. He can rationalize the risk of death to obtain it. Sky divers love to jump. Cops love to chase robbers. If a soldier can rationalize death, then a gambler shooting off his mortgage and car is small potatoes.

The tendency to become addicted to drugs appears to be genetic; it seems to run in families. Alcohol and nicotine are drugs, along with all the rest. A person who tends to have one drug addiction is more likely to have others, more likely to have this one.

I propose that the compulsive gambler is hooked in the same way. His/her need for the drug is sufficient that he/she will rationalize almost any conduct to get it. Being in action produces the drug. The need to be in action reigns supreme.

The money that a gambler risks must be meaningful to him. Suppose you were invited to a poker game in which the stakes were 100 times *smaller* than usual. If you like to play $6-$12, then our game will be 5-cents before the flop and 10-cents after it. Do you think that you could play in that game for five hours ... or even 20 minutes?

This game would be boring, even irritating, to you. There would be no challenge in winning ... no challenge in playing correctly. There would be no danger to you, and no meaningful payoff. This game would not offer you sufficient action and, therefore, no norepinephrine would be produced by your body. If a high-stakes player goes broke, he can get his fix in a smaller game, but the money in the new game then becomes a risk, and therefore acceptable.

Playing too big, not too small, is the pattern. This is the exact reason why players are forever playing in game too big for their bankrolls. Management advice is brushed aside by rationalizing the correctness of entering a game. The same rationalization allows the gambler to risk hundreds, thousands, on games, while at the same time, declining to spend small amounts on family gifts, entertainment, or furniture. To the compulsive gambler, money that is not in action is sort of wasted.

Note that this notion does *not* contend that a gambler plays badly while satisfying the internal need for action. There never was anything to the old rumor that a compulsive gambler "wants to lose." A player entering a big game will be the most alert and quickest-thinking competitor there. He wants to win in the worst way. However, playing over his bankroll carries the seed of disaster when the luck factor runs against him. He simply does not recognize his own false rationalizations that got him into the game in the first place.

To the extent that a compulsive gambler appears to be trying to lose, making many bad bets, one can explain that the game is just too small, and that he soon will move up. He is trying to achieve acceptable action. If he already is in the largest game available, he may continue to play badly until his funds are exhausted. This is one advantage of playing in the biggest game in town: You sometimes will find a player in the game who will go through many thousands of dollars without moving to another game. Smaller games get only a 30-minute look at a person who is on the way up the action ladder. Compulsive gamblers are at your table right now. They are playing the biggest game that they can buy into, and they are trying hard to win.

Keep an eye on your play of garbage hands. If you play them for the action involved — rather than for potential profit — then you are out of the jurisdiction of this book. I predict that in 40 years or so, a medicine or pill will be invented to alleviate the desire for norepinephrine, and that gamblers will be able to deduct it as a business expense.

Bankroll requirements are ignored by anybody who needs them. For what it's worth, I suggest playing in a game where the standard entry amount, not the house minimum, (say, one rack) is within your ability to produce from outside sources on a regular basis. I suggest that you stay in grade until your gambling bankroll is at least 500 times the big blind, and then play higher stakes only with the excess.

Money goes to money, as the saying goes. You might play in a smaller game. But there, you play badly, trying to bet up some action. You then lose to the players who are in danger at that level. Catch 22 — You only play well in a game you cannot afford. Hmmm?

Do you:

(a) Play small and follow a cookbook?

(b) Play in a game you cannot afford, but which contains players who could afford to play even higher? (Hey, I like it!)

(c) Play only in tournaments, where all is even and your entry gives you a chance at big wins while playing desperate chips as the rises come? OK, but between now and Sunday, I could take the thousand to the $15-$30 and ... ♣

# Chapter 26

# Yea, But for the Grace ...

Nobody wants to be on the bricks; nevertheless, it happens. Almost all of the fine players, the big-name players, will tell you that they have lost all their money at one time or another. Some articles on money management have delivered pap, saying that if your bankroll is low, you should play a lower limit. Now, who didn't know that? I mean, if you have lost your money in a big game and no longer have enough to play anymore, it doesn't take a rocket scientist to say, "Play smaller." Reading that advice gives me the feeling that I am a kid being patted on the head.

For what it's worth, here is an idea — maybe right, maybe wrong — on what to do. You have a short budget, but believe that you are a winning player. You intend to play well, to play carefully. Where will that budget have the best chance of survival and small growth?

In the small games of any type of poker ($1-$2, $2-$4, $3-$6, anything below $6-$12 ) where you now are headed, there is a lot of bad play ... a really lot of bad play ... enough bad play to overcome the rake. That bad play comes in the form of players entering too many pots and staying in them too long. This is the key. Take advantage of it.

But wait a minute! Hold'em, "the action game," often rewards people who come in with the worst cards. Hold'em, the action game, often rewards players who stay in pots longer than they should. It happens frequently, and it can last for remarkable streaks. (Remember the statistics I cited earlier which say that a winning player can be behind for more than a year at a time?)

Hold'em is a game that requires a major bankroll if you play it above your replenishment threshold. Stud, "the waiting game," rewards patient play and punishes action seekers. Does it not follow that, to preseve a short bankroll by playing carefully, you should do it in the arena where your intended style of play is rewarded?

Little research on deviation has been done that tells you how big a bankroll you need in the small games. The existing estimates of standard deviation in various poker games are primarily based on professional play in larger games, $15-$30 and up. It may well be true that the deviations in stud at that level are similar to the deviations in hold'em because of the high caliber of play. In my opinion, low-limit hold'em may not be the place to play carefully and survive. The need exists for a proper study of the deviations in these two games at the lower limits.

A perfectly good opposing argument is that, in all small games, the rake is so strong that nobody beats them in the long run. Therefore, your venture is a temporary shot. And therefore, you should play your best game, hold'em. The bad play in low-limit hold'em is terrible ... terrible enough for a good player to have an advantage. Besides, the low-limit stud players know to play tight, tight enough that *nobody* beats the rake. Could be — Is there a statistician out there willing to tackle this problem?

We have all heard of the drunk who looked for his lost keys, not where he had dropped them, but where the light was good enough for him to see. He may not have been right, but he wasn't wrong, either. The light shining for you to seek your lost chips may be shining over the game where your new tight style is fitted to the errors of your opponents. ♣

# Do Not Send To Ask ...

I was playing in a one-table, no-limit hold'em satellite, $60 buy-in as I recall. Play is fast in these things and in some pots, anything can win. One player was a polite young man, not at all the in-your-face type so common for anxious new players. He made a couple of small moves when better ones were available, and I marked him as short on experience.

An hour into the satellite, it got to heads-up and the kid had a slight lead on me. The blinds were huge and a single ace, or anything close to it, was enough for a move. My ace came ... in fact, suited.

I made a big bet which the kid called. The flop made a straight flush and the rest of the chips ran in. A couple of red face cards came and to be polite, I spoke right up — "I have a straight flush."

The kid was staring at his cards and slowly said, "You know, so do I."

Oh well, maybe tomorrow ... ♣

If you intend to play poker for hundreds, maybe thousands, may be millions, then it would be insane not to shell out a couple of hundred for advice. I mean, what other business has such a low overhead? You just might read something that makes a two-hundred buck swing in one pot. Do not skimp.

What to buy and what to think of it? Good question. There is a lot of information out there ... some of it is excellent, some of it isn't, some all ego, and some so simple that you wonder why you spent the money. You may consider, if you like, some thoughts on other writings that impact the hold'em games we play. I like and recommend the following items.

*Super/System.* Doyle Brunson (all honor to his name!) (1979). The best. Is under revision so as to cover new game structure that has evolved since its publication. Contains a good limit hold'em section, although game structure has changed a little. The section on no-limit hold'em is of such high quality that all students of the game pay homage to it. The structure of no-limit hold'em *has not* changed, and there has been no challenge to Brunson's fine instruction. This section alone is worth any book price.

*According to Doyle,* Doyle Brunson (1984). A collection of poker stories and advice. Not an essential to hold'em play, but I'm glad to have read and learned from it.

*Play Poker, Quit Work, and Sleep Till Noon,* John Fox (1977). Written in a five-card draw world, but you can convert to hold'em needs. It contains so many gems of psychology, it simply must be studied. It has 340 pages with only 25 pages on mechanics. The rest is on poker psychology, very real and great instruction. The sections on player image are unmatched.

*The Education of a Poker Player,* Herbert O. Yardley (1957). Serious players have read and learned from this book. A pioneer work in the importance of the psychological aspect of our game.

*Fundamental Secrets of Poker* (1991) and *12 Days to Hold'em Success* (1991), Mike Caro. Excellent goods. My sole caveat is to exclude his trial-balloon idea to limp into hold'em pots. It is guns or knives, high noon in the dirt: Don't limp in!

*The Body Language of Poker (Book of Tells),* (1995), Mike Caro. A fine foray into the psychologies of the game with the only, and therefore the best, photographs. It looks like investment material to me. Caro also has produced a video on the same subject, *Caro's Pro Poker Tells.*

*Poker Probe,* Mike Caro. A software program with which you can compare poker hands on your PC. It runs thousands of comparison deals and gives you the results. Rocks have no need for it, since they already know that an A-K beats a 10-9. We garbage players need to know *how far* our hand is behind, and wouldn't be caught dead without this marvelous tool.

*Tournament Poker* (1995), Tom McEvoy. A thick book with good advice from an experienced tournament winner. Has advice for your specific game. McEvoy kept a little of his best stuff at home, but it was in his first book. Why put money into a tournament without the bargain of his advice and experience?

*Gambling Theory and Other Topics* (1988), Mason Malmuth. Contains necessary material that cannot be found anywhere else. The statistical charts and advice are worth the price.

# ♣ Poker Plus Publications

Poker Plus Publications is dedicated to serving the needs of serious gamblers. Our product list is regularly updated to bring you the best in gambling education, strategy, and entertainment. Books may be ordered directly from Poker Plus Publications, or by Visa/MC from gaming book stores across the nation.

**Tournament Poker (Tom McEvoy)**, 344 pgs, paperback. The long-awaited sequel to 1983 World Series of Poker Champion McEvoy's first tournament book. Tournament Poker outlines winning strategies for all the games in the WSOP. Extensive discussions of 7-card stud, limit hold'em, pot-limit hold'em, no-limit hold'em, Omaha, Omaha high-low, lowball, and razz. Plus rebuy tournaments, satellites, half/half tourneys, and winning conepts for each stage of tournament play. Includes an insightful discussion of the lifestyle and expenses of big-league tournament players. Endorsed by WSOP champions as the "Poker Tournament Bible." $39.95

**Poker Tournament Tips from the Pros (Shane Smith)**, 104 pgs, spiralbound. This well-researched book gives you the winning advice of poker theorists, authors, and tournament winners on the best strategies for winning low-limit rebuy poker tournaments. Smith outlines Top 20 Tips for winning, and lists strategies for each of the 4 Stage of Tournaments. Also includes 26 Tournament Traps and a Poker Potpourri of winning tactics. Opinions of poker luminaries Mike Caro, Bob Ciaffone, Mason Malmuth, Tom McEvoy, and others. A perfect companion book to Tournament Poker. $19.95

**Secrets of Winning Poker (Tex Sheahan**), 200 pgs, paperback. The "dean of poker columnists" leaves this compilation of his best articles as his legacy to poker players. Sheahan gives you sound advice on winning poker strategies for hold'em and stud. Chapters on tournaments, psychology, personality profiles, and some very funny stories from the greenfelt jungle. "Some of the best advice you'll ever read on how to win at poker." (Doyle Brunson) $19.95